Praise for
Keep It Light

"I've been on lots of adventures [...] principles from the trail and ap[...] This book is full of practical a[...] can use to stay strong and keep [...] of life."

—**Mark Batterson,** pastor and bestselling author

"Yes! Amen! *Keep It Light* is practical, powerful, personal, and positive! Joël Malm is a like-minded, God-honoring mentor we would trust to coach and equip anyone who desires to achieve the very best life that God offers. This is a MUST READ for all who want to thrive in life, career, ministry, and relationships."

—**Pam and Bill Farrel,** authors of the bestselling books *Men Are Like Waffles, Women Are Like Spaghetti* and *The 10 Best Decisions a Couple Can Make*

"Joël Malm is a legendary adventurer who has explored some of the most fascinating places on earth, but his greatest discovery isn't anything you can find on a map; it's the discovery of a way of thinking and living that can bring more peace and perspective to your life. In *Keep It Light*, Joël invites you on an adventure of rediscovering what life was really intended to be. I feel lighter and more at peace after reading it, and I'm confident that you will too!"

—**Dave Willis,** author, XO Marriage speaker, and coach

KEEP
IT
LIGHT

KEEP IT LIGHT

The Freedom of Priorities in Life, Work, and Love

Joël Malm

REGNERY
FAITH

Unless otherwise marked, all Scriptures are taken from ESV® Bible (The Holy Bible, English Standard Version®), copyright © 2001 by Crossway, a publishing ministry of Good News Publishers. Used by permission. All rights reserved.

Scriptures marked NIV are taken from the Holy Bible, New International Version®, NIV®. Copyright © 1973, 1978, 1984, 2011 by Biblica, Inc.® Used by permission of Zondervan. All rights reserved worldwide. www.zondervan.com. The "NIV" and "New International Version" are trademarks registered in the United States Patent and Trademark Office by Biblica, Inc.®

Regnery Faith books may be purchased in bulk at special discounts for sales promotion, corporate gifts, fund-raising, or educational purposes. Special editions can also be created to specifications. For details, contact the Special Sales Department, Regnery Faith, 307 West 36th Street, 11th Floor, New York, NY 10018 or info@skyhorsepublishing.com.

Regnery Faith™ is an imprint of Skyhorse Publishing, Inc.®, a Delaware corporation.

Visit our website at www.regnery.com.
Please follow our publisher Tony Lyons on Instagram @tonylyonsisuncertain.

10 9 8 7 6 5 4 3 2 1

Library of Congress Cataloging-in-Publication Data is available on file.

Cover design by Joshua Taggert
Cover photo by Rachael Calk

Print ISBN: 978-1-68451-566-0
Ebook ISBN: 978-1-5107-8151-1

Printed in the United States of America

To Emily and Elise

CONTENTS

CONTENTS

Keeping It Light

A traveler is happier the lighter his load.

—*Marcus Felix*

I lead outdoor expeditions around the world with an organization I started, Summit Leaders. I've taken teams to climb Mt. Kilimanjaro, hike and raft the Grand Canyon, cross the Scottish highlands, walk trails Jesus most assuredly walked across Northern Israel, and hike through the Andes Mountains to the ancient lost city of Machu Picchu.

Most of the people who join me on these trips have never done a major hike before—which is what I want. I'm not looking for people who are all wildernessy and willing to chop off their arm with a Swiss Army knife to survive. Those people would be really out of place on my teams. (Plus, they'd make me look like a wimp!)

Because my teams are all first-timers, they're usually really concerned about having the right gear. I get tons of texts and emails asking questions about exactly what they should bring. So before our trips, I give them a packing list and have them watch a video I recorded about how to pack for a hike. I show them exactly what I bring. I want them to feel confident, but not overpack. But most people still bring way too much with them. Some commission-based salesperson at the outdoor store saw them coming and convinced them they needed every gadget in the store, or else they would die on the mountain. They show up for the hike loaded down with gear.

This is a serious problem.

A pack that's too heavy will wear you out and you won't be able to successfully complete the hike. So I set a weight goal for the bags, and the night before we leave for the trail, I'll often weigh them. If a bag is too heavy, I have that hiker start pulling stuff out.

This process gets highly emotional in a hurry. People get really sensitive about their stuff. I've seen CEOs of large organizations nearly burst into tears when I have them leave some things behind. Some folks even get angry. One girl who I wouldn't let bring a hairdryer was mad at me for days. As I lighten their loads, I can see the fear in their eyes, but I know they'll get over it. Usually by the second day of the hike, those same people thank me for making them lighten their load. They realize just how hard the hike would have been with all that extra weight on their backs.

I'm convinced that nobody intends to overpack. It happens slowly, little by little. We're worried about not having something we may need, so we just take everything. And unintentionally, we end up overloaded and tired, trying to carry a bunch of stuff.

And by the way, I'm not talking about packing for a trip anymore. I'm talking about life.

Life is like a long hike, and most of us are walking along with a pack that feels way too heavy. We're all doing our best to provide for ourselves and our families. We figure if we can just squeeze in a little more, we'll have everything we need. Like a hiker picking up rocks along the trail, thinking we might need them at some point to throw at a bear or lion, we take on more and more. But eventually, we get overloaded.

We're weighed down by financial burdens. We're doing all we can to provide for our families and give our kids what we never had growing up, but it seems impossible to get ahead. Just when we think there might be some breathing room, a major expense arises—a car or appliance breaks down, a medical emergency. It feels like we always need just a little more to feel secure and comfortable.

We're weighed down by demands on our time. Work deadlines, overtime, kids' sports schedules. We feel like slaves to our schedules, with no time to just relax. When there is a moment to relax, we feel guilty, thinking surely we're dropping one of the many balls we're juggling. Sometimes we get so used to being busy that not being busy feels awkward and uncomfortable.

We're weighed down by things that consume our energy—important projects, kids' extracurricular events, and the maintenance we have to do just to keep life from falling apart. Add to that all the things that sap our emotional energy—relational conflict, responsibilities, seeking others' approval, managing their expectations and opinions. They all take a toll on our physical and emotional well-being and leave us, well . . . tired. I heard someone say, "The world is run by tired people." Basically, yes—it is. If we could take an entire day to sleep, most of us would—but anxiety and stress actually keep most of us from sleeping soundly, making us even more tired!

Maybe for you, things are under control most of the time, but there's conflict you keep bumping up against. The disagreements with your spouse about money—whether to save or spend. The ongoing discussions and subtle hints being dropped about how you or those you love spend their time.

Or maybe it's the periodic "crashes" you experience (seemingly out of nowhere) when you find yourself in bed, wiped out, spending days trying to recover and get back to normal. You feel like a failure when you're forced to stop moving. The weight of those periodic meltdowns is taking its toll.

If we're honest, most of us feel that the weight of life is a lot heavier than we'd like it to be. And we aren't quite sure how to lighten it. We'd like to, but it seems impossible or reckless to stop carrying some things. A lot of what we we're carrying is actually good stuff—opportunities, relationships. But as the weight builds, we feel overwhelmed, like we're carrying around a giant pack. We're strong, but not that strong. Eventually, we end up dreading every day, saying, "I'm tired and I can't carry all this anymore."

We read in the Bible where Jesus says, "My burden is light,"[1] but how many of us actually feel like the burden of life is light? Is this just something nice that Jesus said so we can put it on inspirational cards and memes? Or is it possible that He was serious and maybe—just maybe—we need to evaluate exactly why we aren't feeling the lightness He talked about?

I'm convinced that Jesus really meant what He said and, if we get intentional about it, we can actually experience that lightness. But it won't happen by default, mostly because we live in a world that will naturally push us to carry more and more.

This is a book about how to be strategic and make sure you're only carrying what you need to live a life that honors God. My goal is to offer some insights I've learned along the way that I believe can actually help you experience the lightness Jesus was talking about. It really is possible to have the time and energy you want to give to those you love the most. It's possible to have less and actually be more content. It's possible to not feel constantly short on resources and in constant fear of lack. But it will take intentionality. Freedom comes when we prioritize the right things.

And here's some good news: Most of the time, it doesn't require totally overhauling your life. It usually just takes a few tweaks here and there, plus a shift in mindset. Keeping it light isn't about doing more; it's about making sure you're only carrying what is absolutely necessary for the journey ahead.

The Path toward the Light

Jesus wants to lighten the load you're carrying. He says, "Come to me, all who labor and are heavy laden, and I will give you rest. Take my yoke upon you . . . For my yoke is easy, and my burden is light."[2] A yoke is a large piece of wood that was placed over the shoulders of two oxen. Those oxen would pull a heavy burden together. They shared the load because it was a lot to pull. But they had to work together. If one got ahead of the other, they'd end up pulling more weight on their own. Balance and power came when they walked in lockstep.

Jesus says that if you want to lighten your load in life, get connected with Him. Take His yoke. You still have to carry something, but doing it with Him will make it bearable. We all have a unique burden of responsibility to carry, but that burden gives life meaning. Kids, jobs, and relationships can be really challenging sometimes—but they also bring the greatest fulfillment and a sense of purpose. Trying to carry no burden at all will only lead to feeling like life is meaningless.

But if the burden of life seems too heavy to bear, there's a good chance you're carrying something you weren't meant to carry alone (or at all). And it's creating unnecessary suffering.

Some suffering is just part of life. "We must go through many hardships to enter the kingdom of God."[3] (I wish that verse weren't in there.) God uses that kind of suffering to strengthen us and help us grow. It's necessary suffering. It makes us "strong in the Lord and in his mighty power."[4] We know this instinctively when it comes to physical strength. The only way to get stronger physically is to push yourself slightly beyond what you think you can handle, little by little—no pain, no gain. That principle applies in our spiritual lives, too. Suffering builds strength.

But no one gets started on a path to strength at the gym

by lifting four-hundred-pound weights in their first workout. You'll never get the weight off the ground and will probably hurt yourself in the process! Lifting something you can't actually carry won't make you stronger—it just crushes you. Only lifting what you can actually lift, in increasing increments, will make you stronger. The same is true in life, work, and love.

When we carry the burden God asks of us—our responsibility—it makes us stronger. But when it comes to a really heavy weight that we can't carry on our own, we trust that His strength will be there to help us with that burden. That's what Paul was talking about when he said suffering "produces endurance, and endurance produces character, and character produces hope."[5] Carrying the burden we are called to carry offers the hope of meaning and purpose. That's the necessary suffering that leads to strength.

But adding things God never intended for us to carry—or trying to do life in our own way—creates unnecessary suffering. It's exhausting and overwhelming. Sometimes we think we're pleasing God by going above and beyond what He asks. Sometimes we're carrying things that have slowly accumulated and we don't even realize they are holding us back. Not only does that suffering not help us grow, it actually hinders our forward movement. And it creates all sorts of chaos.

We naturally tend to complicate things in life. It's human nature to go outside the simplicity of what God asks of us. He made one simple request of Adam and Eve: Do not eat of the fruit of the Tree of the Knowledge of Good and Evil. But when the serpent asked Eve what God had commanded, she added her own twist to it: She said she wasn't supposed to eat it, *or even touch it.* The original sin that got us into this mess came when we started adding stuff to God's simple request.

Spiritual maturity comes when we carry what is ours to carry and learn to trust God with what isn't ours to carry.

It's learning to stay in lockstep with Him. If we rush ahead, we'll end up carrying more than we're meant to carry. If we pull to the side or lag behind (out of fear of what's ahead), we'll also end up carrying too much of the burden. But when we walk at Jesus's pace and take no more than what has been placed on our shoulders, it keeps the weight of life light.

The challenging thing is, this isn't a one-time decision. It takes constant evaluation. What we should be carrying at any given time is a constantly moving target based on the season of life we're in. There's a burden and a blessing for each season of life. Maturity is learning to embrace the blessing and shoulder only the burden God is asking you to carry in each season.

This is why, from time to time, you need to stop and evaluate what needs to have priority on this stage of your journey. Like a hiker packing for a trip, what we put in our bag depends on where we're planning to go. Which is why, before you load up your bag, you should always start by defining your destination.

Define the Destination

You don't pack flip-flops to climb through the snows of Mt. Kilimanjaro. You don't take a goose-down parka for a trek through the Amazon. Life is no different. When you know where you're going, it's a lot easier to know what you need and don't need—which is why it's really important to define your destination in life. You need to figure out where you want to go.

After working with lots of people over the years, I've

found that most know what they *don't* want more than what they *do* want. They may have a vague idea of what they think they want, but it often has more to do with running from what they don't want.

I don't want to be poor.

I don't want to be insignificant.

I don't want to be alone.

When you know what you *don't* want more than what you *do* want, you'll find yourself reacting to life most of the time. You'll settle for anything that offers to instantly take away the discomfort you don't want to feel. You'll be moving all the time, but you'll be running away with no direction. You can run *from* something in any direction. But you can only run *toward* something in one direction.

If you're running from being poor, you'll work with no financial goal in mind other than: *a little more.*

If you're running from feeling insignificant, anything that gives a quick moment of feeling important—likes on social media, relational drama—will drive you.

If you're running from being alone, you'll end up using time and energy to win over people you don't even like so you won't feel alone.

It's good to know what you don't want. But a big part of having a vision for your life is getting a clear picture of what you actually *do* want. When you know where you're going, you'll know exactly what to bring and what can be left behind.

That's what King Solomon was talking about when he said, "Where there is no prophetic vision the people cast off restraint."[6] When you don't know exactly where you're going, you'll just throw everything into your bag. But when you have a clear picture of your final destination—a vision for the future—you'll pack only what you need to get you where you want to go. You'll give valuable space in your bag to only what's most important.

So, to do a good gear check on your life, you need to evaluate what's important to you.

A Question of Values

People often tell me, "I really want to travel more, but it's so expensive. How can you afford to travel so much?" They look at my fifteen-year-old, beat-up car and the tiny house I live in, and it seems pretty clear I'm not rolling in money. And they are correct to think that. But that old car and small home are a big part of the reason I *can* afford to travel so much.

Having a nice, new car isn't that important to me, but travel is. So rather than making a car payment every month, I take what I would have spent on that and divide it into savings—a little for travel and a little for when my family will need a new (to us, but in reality, older) car. We've also decided to live in a house that is way less than what we can afford. When we travel, we do it inexpensively by going with friends and splitting costs. In fact, the amount of money most people would use for four months of car payments (or a few days at a theme park in Florida or California) will get us two weeks in Europe.

There is absolutely nothing wrong with having a nice, dependable vehicle. (Honestly, sometimes we do get a little jealous of people with nice, shiny cars with no dents in them.) And there's nothing wrong with having a big, beautiful home. It's just that travel is more important to us than those things, so we put our money, time, and energy toward it.

We all have certain things that we value—a nice home, a secure job, loving relationships, respect—and we instinctively give our time, money, and energy to those things.

Values are unique to each person, and there is an unlimited number of things you can value. Some of our values are learned through the way we were raised. Some are just adopted, without much question, based on the society or culture we live in. And the truth is, many of our values come from doing whatever it takes to make sure the thing we fear the most doesn't come upon us.

That's part of what Jesus was talking about when He said: "Where your treasure is, there will your heart be also."[7] If you want to know what your heart is set on (what you value), look at what you do with your time, money, and energy (your treasures). If you want to know what someone really values, look at what they do—not what they say or think or feel.

If you voluntarily work a lot of hours, there's a good chance achievement or financial security are probably things you value highly.

If you engage in all sorts of online debates and always want the latest gossip, then—like it or not—drama and conflict might be of high value for you.

If you work out a lot, fitness, health, or how you look is of high value.

As I said, I drive an old car. As much as I would love to travel and also be able to drive a new car, my bank account tells me that's just not possible. I've only got so much income and so much money.

And this is the challenge we all eventually face: We are limited. And as a result, at some point the things we value come into conflict with each other. We have to decide what will get our best resources of time, money, and energy. Not every value can have equal value. If everything has the same value, nothing has value. You can be certain that if you're trying to give everything equal value—i.e., put it all in your backpack—you'll quickly get overwhelmed and frustrated.

We need to have an order—a hierarchy—to our values. Sometimes we have to sacrifice one value to give our best to another.

When life changes—you get married, have kids, change jobs, a relationship ends, kids leave the house—you'll need to make some changes to your value structure. If you're still doggedly pursuing goals that you set for yourself in your teens, twenties, or thirties without adjusting for new values that have appeared since then—like kids and a spouse—there's a good chance some of your more recent values may suffer as a result. If you're still trying to keep the same pace you did years ago, without accounting for the reality of your current energy level or responsibilities, you'll get frustrated and exhausted.

Some values must change with new seasons. That's why it's so important to get really clear about what you value most and prioritize what to put in your backpack for this stage of the journey. Making the right sacrifice ensures that we keep it light on the part we're walking right now.

How do you know if a value needs to change? Great question. Fortunately, there's a pretty simple answer: tension. When you feel the weight of relational tension, frustration, or irritation in yourself or from others, it's a sign that you may need to change some priorities to make sure you're only carrying what you need for this phase of your journey. In a strange way, tension can actually become a gift that helps you properly prioritize what's most important in this season.

And that's what we'll talk about next.

2

Priorities

*Perfection is attained not when there is
nothing more to add, but when there is
nothing more to remove.*

—*Antoine de Saint-Exupéry*

I had no idea how bad things had gotten. In fact, I actually thought things had never been better.

As my wife, Emily, and I strolled our six-month-old daughter through a beautiful, wooded park one Monday morning, I felt so grateful. "Isn't it so amazing that I can spend a weekday morning walking with you?" I commented. "No boss telling me to get to work. Money is rolling in. I'm feeling super fulfilled. This is really working out well for us."

Emily was silent for a moment. "I don't know," she said. "I feel kind of alone and abandoned."

Excuse me? "Abandoned? By who?"

She wouldn't look me in the eye. "You."

"What are you talking about?! I'm at home all the time. I built this whole business to give me freedom to work from home and have the extra money I knew we'd need when our daughter was born."

"Yeah. You've been really successful but you're always working, and I feel alone."

I was really irritated. How dare she feel alone! It seemed pretty clear to me what was work and what wasn't—and I was *home* all the time now.

"Emily," I said, "I did all this for you and our daughter."

"Did you?" she asked. "Or were you just freaking out that we wouldn't have the money we needed when the baby came along?"

I was furious. I had worked hard and made some major sacrifices to make sure I was home more. Before then, I'd been gone for multiple weeks at a time, several times every year, leading outdoor expeditions around the world in Africa, South America, and Asia. But I knew that when our daughter was born, I'd need to be around more, so I hustled to build what was stacking up to be a very successful leadership coaching business. It was a lot of pressure and took constant work, but I actually enjoyed it. It brought money and freedom, and I was at home. It was all working perfectly in my mind.

Which is why I could not believe what I was hearing.

As the conversation continued, I found myself getting increasingly irritated. I felt like my wife was ungrateful for all the hard work and sacrifices I was making for our family. But at the same time, that conversation was a wake-up call for me. I realized that even if I was having major success in other areas, if things weren't good at home, it didn't matter that much. Every area of our lives—family, finances, and career—tends to be connected. When one thing is out of balance, it begins to affect the rest.

The more questions I asked Emily, the more I realized that things really had gotten out of balance, and I needed to reevaluate my priorities.

I'm gonna go out on a limb here and guess that you probably picked up this book because there's a bit of tension in your life right now. Something or someone has made you aware that your life might be a bit out of balance. Or maybe you're sick of feeling overwhelmed and tired, and you want to know what to do about that. Most people don't pick up books about prioritizing things in their life unless:

A. They feel overwhelmed and unhappy that they don't have time, money, or energy to do what they really value most.

Or, like me . . .

B. Someone has made you aware that *they* aren't happy about how little of you is available to them.

In any given moment of life, there is likely to be some tension. We all tend to have at least one area of our life where we feel blocked, with limits that we just can't seem to overcome. I'm convinced that those tension points can be a gift, if we'll pay attention.

Here are some common tension points I've heard from people over the years:

- There seems to be no time for what I really want to do.
- I feel like my energy is constantly sapped and I have nothing left to give to the people and activities I really love.
- I'm constantly overwhelmed by money issues. I make decent money, but it feels like I'm never able to round the corner and find the financial freedom I want.

- I just got jolted when a relationship in my life fell apart, seemingly out of nowhere, all because the person who left said I wasn't giving them what they needed.
- I'm in the throes of regret over what I lost right now, and am wondering where things went wrong. I'm hoping and praying there's some way to get back what I've lost.

If you're feeling any of those tension points, let me tell you: You aren't alone. I've worked with people from all walks of life—CEOs, not-for-profit leaders, pastors, and housewives—who all hit a tension point and realized something needed to change. What I'm about to share is the very practical process I walk them through (it's also the process I personally use at the beginning of every year) to manage those tension points and lighten the load so my clients and I can give our best to what matters most.

The big questions to start with are: What do you need to let go of that is holding you back? What do you need to sacrifice in this season?

The Right Sacrifice

I think it's pretty fascinating that the first time we read about relational tension between humans in the Bible is also the first time we read about sacrifice.

In Genesis, Cain and his brother Abel both bring a sacrifice to God. For some reason, God rejects Cain's sacrifice. This makes Cain angry at God. (But then he takes it out on his brother, as we often tend to do—take our frustration with life out on others.)

God asks him, "Why are you angry, and why has your face fallen? If you do well, will you not be accepted? And if you do not do well, sin is crouching at the door. Its desire is contrary to you, but you must rule over it."[1]

The word translated "sin" (*chata*) in this verse comes from an archery term that means "to miss the mark." God basically tells Cain that he misses the mark because he was aiming at the wrong thing. God didn't value what Cain valued, so He didn't accept his sacrifice.

It's a hard pill to swallow, but it's important to understand: There are wrong sacrifices.

I talk to people all the time who realize, too late, that they sacrificed their marriage for their career or ministry. Hospitals are filled with people who sacrificed their health for the sake of pleasure and convenience. I've seen friends sacrifice a healthy, life-giving community for a pay increase in their job that required them to move away. Lots of people sacrifice their long-term relationship with their kids in the name of providing financial security for them. They spend hours away from their families to provide money, but what the family really wants is their presence. Provision is more than just money.

Here's the *really* hard pill to swallow: You can be sincere, honest, live a morally upright life—be faithful to your wife, pay your taxes, provide for your family—but if you value the wrong things, you can end up feeling the same negative results of remorse and regret as if you had committed a horrible, actual sin.

A pastor recently shared with me that he resented his ex-wife for leaving him. He humbly bragged about how he had been faithful to her, prayed for her, and loved her. He made lots of sacrifices to be in the ministry. He was angry at her and the kids for not supporting the "call" on his life. But his wife was angry, too. She said he prioritized ministry to others ahead of caring for his own family. After some soul-searching, the pastor admitted that he had sacrificed his family for the affirmation he got from always being available to his church. He made a lot of sacrifices for ministry, but he sacrificed the wrong things.

For the record, if you feel like your spouse or kids are getting in the way of your goals—whether they involve ministry, business, or something else—there's a good chance your values might be out of line and you're in the process of making the wrong sacrifice. It's possible to be very sincere and loyal to those you love but still make the wrong sacrifice. You can aim wrong. You have to keep a constant eye on whether or not what you are really sacrificing for is truly of highest value.

What makes this even more challenging is the fact that values tend to change as we go through life. Some values shouldn't ever change (more on that shortly), but many need to be adjusted based on the season of life you're in. The right sacrifice is often a moving target.

A Moving Target

Before I had that enlightening (and jolting) conversation with Emily, I was getting angry a lot after our daughter was born.

I wasn't hitting things or yelling at people, but I struggled with the kind of anger that sits just below the surface, ready to erupt—sometimes at the smallest frustrations. Autocorrect would presumptuously change what I had written, and I'd want to throw my phone across the office. I'd bump my head and want to scream. I didn't take it out on people, but I hated always feeling like I was about to snap. I knew that something not good—tension—was building inside me.

Looking back, I see that the conversation with Emily was the catalyst that made me wake up to a reality I would have preferred to ignore: Having a kid changes *every*thing.

Our lives had completely changed, but I was still trying to live the same way I always had. Emily and I used to travel all over the place on a whim. (She's a flight attendant, so it was easy to just pick a flight that had open seats and take off.) We always had tons of flexibility. Also, I prided myself on being efficient. I was able to get a lot of stuff done in one day. I also used to be able to sleep. All that changed the day our daughter was born.

I understood on a mental level that life changes when you have kids, but I thought I was invincible. I figured if I just pushed a little harder or used brute force, I could still cram everything I had been doing into a day, even with a child in tow. I hadn't actually changed anything in my life; I just added a new value to the bag and kept charging ahead. I was still mentally trying to live by an old value system.

That value system worked great before I had a kid, but the season had changed. A new value—a big one, my daughter—came in and took the place of traveling, productivity, flexibility, and sleep. Using my time, energy, and money in the same way as before she was born left me tired and frustrated.

When seasons change, value systems have to be re-e-**value**-ated.

King Solomon said there's a season for everything in life.[2] Every season requires different resources. We understand this when it comes to summer and winter, but it also applies in seasons of life. What's important in one season may not be quite as important—or even unwise to keep with us—in another. Life is constantly changing, and if we don't adapt, we will just have constant frustration with ourselves and those around us.

After Emily and I had that conversation at the park, I did some soul-searching. I decided I needed to write down what was most important in that season of life. This is the values hierarchy, or order, I developed for myself:

My values right now:

1. Relationship with God
2. Being present for my wife
3. Being present for my daughter
4. Caring for my health
5. Providing financially

When I was honest about why I was working so much, I realized that Emily was right about it being based in fear. I had no idea what a child would cost, so my concern about not having enough money was driving me to give more of myself to a lesser value. Providing financially (number 5 on the list) was getting more of my time and energy than a higher value—being present for my wife (number 2 on the list). That was the tension point. In Emily's eyes, she was being sacrificed for something of lesser value. I circled that tension point and set out to do whatever it took to set things in the right order.

My values right now:

1. Relationship with God

2. Being present for my wife

3. Being present for my daughter

4. Caring for my health

5. Providing financially

That tension point with Emily actually became a gift. It was like a warning sign on the journey of life. Tension points cause us to pay attention and adjust accordingly.

When we start to experience negative emotions like frustration, disappointment, or irritation with ourselves or those around us, it's easy to ignore them. Who likes negative emotions? It's easier to just push ahead. But those emotions are like road signs. We ignore them at our peril.

Now, don't get me wrong. Emotions can lie. They are bad guides for how to live our lives, but they are great signs that help make us aware of things we may have missed. They give us important cues that can help guide our relationships and navigate new terrain. If you're feeling an uncomfortable emotion, don't ignore it—explore it!

Heeding the Signs

I recently shared this material with a large group, and afterward, a successful engineer told me about a tension point she was dealing with. After twelve years of balancing her work with single motherhood, she had recently gotten married. For the last twelve years, her son and her job had been two of her highest values. But now her new husband had entered her value system. She was only a few months into the marriage, but she was getting into lots of arguments with him—mostly revolving around him feeling like he was coming in second place to her son.

She had some pretty solid logic for that: "I know God says my husband needs to be first. But he may leave me, like the last guy did," she said. "My son will always be my son."

Deep down, this woman was afraid that if she spent more of her time and energy on her new husband, her son would resent her for it. And if her new husband eventually left, she'd lose *everything* she valued.

Understandably, rearranging her values was scary. Making the right sacrifice can be a true test of faith. But finding balance and keeping it light always requires a right sacrifice when life changes and new values come into the mix.

Marriage requires new sacrifices. I've talked to newly-weds who complain that their spouse is still living like a single person—hanging out with friends, without their spouse, until late in the night. It creates resentment because one partner didn't change his or her value system after the wedding.

Kids require tons of sacrifice. Caring for them can be all-consuming. We have to make sure that we don't sacrifice our spouse for our kids. The kids will leave the house one day, but you'll want your spouse around until death do you part.

Family time requires sacrifice. I can't tell you how many parents I meet who are tired and resentful because of their kids' sports schedules and after-school activities. They feel like they're driving all over creation all the time. There's nothing wrong with activities, but when they intrude on higher values, you can be sure it will cause some irritation—and probably some exhaustion. We only have our kids for a short time, which is why those résumé-building extracurricular activities they're involved in sometimes need to be sacrificed: They've slipped in and eroded the important values of family time and involvement in church.

There will be times that we have to let go of good, fun things because they're just causing too much strain or taking us away from something far more important, like spiritual growth or relational strength. But if you are sacrificing something because you are living by higher values, you can lay your head to rest at night with a sense of peace—you lived by your values. No, the porch didn't get painted this weekend, but you finally got to spend some quality time with your increasingly elusive teenage daughter. She'll be out of the house sooner than you know it, and you can paint the porch after that! You didn't get the extra money for working all weekend, but you went to the men's event at your church and realized some things you can do to improve your marriage.

When you aim at the right thing for this season, you can be certain that in the long run, you'll love the results.

The Highest Aim

I wish I could tell you that, after all the travel I've done, I don't overpack my bags. But I still do. I usually have the packing under control until right before I leave, but at the last minute I think: *What if I need* _____? Usually, I don't actually need that thing. I tend to come home from the trip with lots of stuff I never used at all. The worst part is, I usually don't have room to bring back anything new because my bags are already full when I go.

Such is the nature of life. We all tend to worry that we aren't going to have something we need. We have a hard time sacrificing.

Fortunately, we have a Guide who knows what we really will need in life. He sees what's ahead. When we learn to trust His packing list, we'll be able to keep it light. Jesus understood the challenge of being human, the fear and anxiety we all feel about not having something we'll need. He said:

> "So do not worry, saying, 'What shall we eat?' or
> 'What shall we drink?' or 'What shall we wear?'
> For the pagans run after all these things, and your
> heavenly Father knows that you need them. But

seek first his kingdom and his righteousness, and all these things will be given to you as well."[3]

God made you. He knows what you need. But He says if you want those things, don't seek those things. Set your sights on something higher. Seek His kingdom.

God's kingdom is His order; it's valuing what He values. He made everything "in heaven and on earth, visible and invisible, whether thrones or dominions or rulers or authorities—all things were created through him and for him."[4] He made us and knows what will bring us the most peace and fulfillment. Seeking the Kingdom of God is how we live in harmony with the seen and unseen realities of our existence. It's also how we get a clear packing list for every season and stage of life.

Jesus was the living example of what it looks like to live out that Kingdom on Earth. His life, death, and resurrection showed us what the freedom of living by God's priorities looks like. If we want that freedom, we have to prioritize what Jesus did.

So what did He value most?

Jesus kept the packing list pretty simple. When a wealthy

young man approached Him and asked for the bottom
line—what was most important in life—He narrowed it
down to this: Love God and love people. That's the simple
hierarchy of what God values:

　　1. God

　　2. People

Wanting God's way above our way should always be first.
Anything else we desire—money, work, health,
success—should be prioritized as lesser values. This means
sacrificing our desires for His desires. That's a big part of
what the Apostle Paul was talking about when he said,
"Therefore, I urge you, brothers and sisters, in view of God's
mercy, to offer your bodies as a living sacrifice, holy and
pleasing to God—this is your true and proper worship."[5] Our
highest priority is lining our lives up with what God values.

Our second highest value should always be people.
Anything that gets in the way of relationships with people
should always be of less importance—which is why relationships tend to create the most tension points for us. If you
think about it, the heaviest weight we carry tends to be relational pressure. Work gets busy and challenging, but we can
shoulder that load if we have good support in that season.

Illness is hard, but it's worse when we have to carry it alone. When you've got a supporting family or friends, it makes the burden much lighter.

If you're going to keep it light, relationships need to be a priority. Relationship with God first and relationship with people second. Relationships always require sacrifice. In some seasons, relationships with our spouse and kids will require sacrificing things we really enjoy. But if we make the right sacrifice, in line with what God values, then God can take that sacrifice and make something amazing from it. In fact, if you make the right sacrifice, there's a very good chance that the things you sacrificed will come back to life in a more glorious form later down the road.

Let me explain.

Resurrecting the Sacrifice

My friend Misty is a brilliant woman with lots of drive who had big hopes and dreams for her career. But when she felt like God told her to lay down those dreams to raise her children, she did it. She stayed home and raised her kids—even homeschooling them. But as the last kids were preparing to graduate from high school, she felt God reignite something in her heart.

She started a Christian podcast conference and network called Spark Media. In no time, God propelled her to the national stage as a voice for Christian podcasting. Despite the fact that her first podcast conference happened just days before the COVID pandemic lockdowns started, God has been exponentially blessing that ministry. God has done in a few short years what it takes many people decades to build, and I'm convinced it's because Misty obeyed what she felt He was asking of her. She made the sacrifice, seemingly letting her dreams die, and then God chose to resurrect them.

This is His pattern. Death first, then resurrection in a more glorious form. But you don't get a glorious resurrection without a sacrifice and the death of something. Jesus lived out that pattern and set the greatest example of this: God loved the world (people) so much that He gave (sacrificed) His only Son, so whoever believes in Him would not perish, but have everlasting life.[6]

When I think back to the order of my top three highest values—God, my wife, and my daughter—I realize that God set that order first. God's people, the Church, are called the

Bride of Christ. It's pretty mind-blowing to think about, but you and I are so valuable that God sacrificed His Son for us.

But that wasn't the end: The very thing He sacrificed was brought back to life in a more glorious form.

Don't be surprised if you sacrifice a dream in this season only to find that God resurrects that dream later in life. It's never too late. One touch of God's favor can change everything in an instant. He can bring it back to life. But it starts when you value what He values—in the order He values it. It starts when we sacrifice our desires for His priorities and let go of things that are of lesser value.

You have no idea what's waiting on the other side of your willingness to make the right sacrifice for this season.

Taking Aim

If something in your life is creating relational tension or frustration, don't just tolerate it. And please don't ignore it! Evaluate it and make the necessary changes. Figure out where values are competing and creating exhaustion and stress. Then make the sacrifice necessary to bring balance and peace.

You can't carry it all. You only have so much time, money,

and energy. What will you leave behind today? What are you going to take out of your pack that snuck in there? What are you still trying to carry that has outlived its use? What are you going to stop doing? What are you going to let go of?

It may be scary. You may have to lay down some values you've held onto since your teens or twenties. The sacrifice may seem too much. It may feel irresponsible to let go. If may feel like you've failed. But I'm convinced you can't actually sacrifice for God. He won't let you. The minute you think you've given something up in the name of valuing what He values, He'll open the windows of Heaven and pour out blessings you never could have imagined.

It won't be a sacrifice.

3

Focus

*Look for yourself, and you will find in the long
run only hatred, loneliness, despair, rage, ruin,
and decay. But look for Christ and you will find
Him, and with Him everything else thrown in.*

—C. S. Lewis

I spent my teens living in Guatemala. But when I was fifteen, we came back to Texas, and I spent a summer learning to drive. My grandpa would take me out onto some narrow country backroads in his little truck and turn me loose. I got the hang of driving pretty quickly, but I would always panic when a large truck would come barreling toward me. I was constantly watching the lines on the road, but regularly found myself driving over the shoulder or sometimes into the middle lane when a car was coming at me until my dad finally told me, as calmly as possible: "You tend to move toward what you're focused on. Don't look at the lines or the cars coming at you. Pick a point in the distance and focus on that. You'll naturally stay between the lines."

It worked. The more I focused on something ahead, the more I naturally stayed in my lane and didn't panic about cars coming at me. This skill came in handy when we went back to Guatemala, because at the time, there were no lines on the roads. It was a free-for-all. You *really* had to pick something in the distance to focus on there because there wasn't a lot of clarity about where you should be.

King Solomon said, "Where there is no prophetic vision the people cast off restraint."[1] A prophetic vision is simply a picture of what the future could look like—something to aim at. It's starting with a goal in mind. Without something ahead to focus your attention on, you'll easily get distracted by what's closest or coming at you fastest. And you'll never know when you've arrived.

We all need something to aim at and move toward in life. Most of us have a vague picture of what we want, but that vision tends to be more focused on what we *don't* want—because we've seen that. We know what it looks like. But it can be hard to envision a future we've never actually seen.

C. S. Lewis describes our shortsighted tendencies this way:

> We are half-hearted creatures, fooling about with drink and sex and ambition when infinite joy is offered us, like an ignorant child who wants to go on making mud pies in a slum because he cannot imagine what is meant by the offer of a holiday at the sea. We are far too easily pleased.[2]

We just don't know what we don't know. For many of us, our primary focus is on not getting hit by oncoming traffic or driving off the road, but God has something way bigger for us than just survival! He has greater plans for you than you even have for yourself!

Our own desires for the future can easily sell us short. You've probably also noticed that our desires change over time. What we want now may be completely different in another season. We can spend years pouring our efforts into what we think we want and find that, once we have it, it wasn't all it was cracked up to be. So we end up wanting more, or different things. Thomas Merton compared it to climbing a ladder then realizing the ladder was up against the

wrong wall the whole time. Bottom line: Our shortsighted-
ness and fickle desires tend to sell us short on all God has for
us and says we can be.

Since we don't know what we don't know, we don't know
what could be, and we don't even know what we really want
a lot of the time, Jesus offers the answer: Seek the
Kingdom—His order. Make His Kingdom your fixed point
of focus, and God promises He'll give you what your heart
really desires.

God knows what will truly fulfill you. He made you. He
knows exactly what you need to become all He intends for
you to be. That's why King David said, "Delight yourself in
the Lord, and he will give you the desires of your heart."[3]

But he's not talking about getting that Tesla you've been
eyeing or the romantic partner you dreamed of; he's talking
about getting what God knows will really bring you fulfillment. What we desire tends to be shortsighted and misguided.
What you want for yourself is small. When you seek what
God values as your primary focus, you'll get what you really
want, but probably don't even realize you want it until then.
His plan for your life is what you would want your plan to
be if you knew all the details.

When we stay focused on seeking His Kingdom, He gives us what our hearts really desire.

You'll notice Jesus directed us to *seek* the Kingdom, not *find*. There's a profound truth in that choice of words. From a psychological standpoint, human happiness and fulfillment tends to be the result of moving toward a desired goal—not actually from attaining it. Happiness is a byproduct of right pursuit. Happiness (or perhaps a better word is "joy") comes from pursuing the right goal. The higher your goal, the greater your chances of finding joy in its pursuit.

And there's no higher goal in life than seeking the Kingdom of God.

When we constantly seek what God values, we find success—which is why success is a direction, not a destination. Success happens when we pour our focus into seeking God's Kingdom and what He values. The natural byproduct is joy and fulfillment.

There are no limits to where God can take you if you make His Kingdom your highest goal—no matter what your specific job or calling may be in this season. So your job is simply this: Focus on doing your best to honor God with whatever He has given you. The Bible calls this stewardship, and it's how we keep it light while pursuing a vision for our lives.

God has given you the resources you need to arrive at the destiny He has for you. You may feel limited or inadequate, but know this: You have what you need, right now, to get where He wants to take you. Your job is to stay focused on what you have—not on what you don't have. Focusing on what we don't have, or what others have that we don't, just makes our burden a lot heavier. Stay in your lane, aimed at using your resources for God's Kingdom, and you can be certain you'll get where you really want to go.

In my experience, there are two specific things He has given us that can take us places we never dreamed if we steward them well: 1) our innate abilities, and 2) our treasure (time, money, and energy).

So let's look at how to really stay focused on using what we have to the best of our ability, believing God "is able to do far more abundantly than all that we ask or think, according to the power at work within us."[4]

Use What You've Got

When I got my master's degree in counseling, a career counselor told me a handful of things I could do with it. Problem was, I didn't like any of those things! I had taken a break from leading outdoor expeditions—something I really loved—to get that degree. Now, I was being told that the jobs I could get with it all involved sitting in an office. I hate offices, but I started to come to terms with the idea that I might have to do outdoor adventures on the side while I worked from an office.

Rather than just resign myself to an office job, though, I started seeking counsel and asking God what He wanted me to do. The general direction I heard was, "Use what you already have." I did. I went back to leading adventures, even though it felt like I had wasted lots of time, money, and energy getting that degree. But God knew what He was doing.

There was no way I (or anyone else, for that matter) could have seen the path He would lead me on. In a very real way, I *am* doing counseling, but it's in a context I love that fits perfectly with my personality. That degree has come in super handy in my coaching and leadership training, but the way God chose to use it wasn't on any list at the career counselor's office. Who'd have thought that degree would have me leading outdoor adventures, writing books, coaching leaders, and speaking all over the country?

God knew exactly what would bring fulfillment in my life; I didn't. But in seeking Him, I found what I really wanted. And He keeps on unfolding His plan in my life with one thing building on the last.

The same is true for you.

God knows how He made you. He knows *why* He made you. You "are his workmanship, created in Christ Jesus for good works, which God prepared beforehand, that [you] should walk in them."[5] You have a specific mission to fulfill as you seek His Kingdom in your life. You've been given some very specific tools to accomplish that mission. You may not know where the road is going to lead you, but if you'll stay faithful with what He has given you, you can be certain good things are ahead.

You have what you need, right now, to accomplish the mission He has given you—not the whole mission, but the part of the journey you're on right now. You don't need more; you just need to make sure you're using what you have to the best of your ability. When you use what He has given you while seeking His Kingdom, even if it seems small or insufficient, you can be sure you'll find fulfillment and please God in the process.

When Jesus talked about how things work when we're seeking God's Kingdom, He told a parable about a man who left three of his servants with money (talents) before he went on a trip.[6] Two of the servants doubled the money he gave them while he was gone. But the third one buried his money because he was scared of failing. When the master got back, he was pretty disappointed with the one who hadn't increased what he had been given. He said, "You ought to have invested my money with the bankers, and at my coming I should have received what was my own with interest."[7] He then takes the money from that servant and gives it to the one who had made the most money from the initial investment.

In the parable, the master is really harsh to that scared guy. But Jesus wants to drive something home: In God's kingdom, we're expected to build on what He has given us. Breaking even isn't enough.

I think we can all relate to that servant who hid what he had out of fear. It can be scary to start using what God has given us. *What if we mess it up or fail?* It's easy to get paralyzed into inaction. Sometimes we feel like we need more training or someone's stamp of approval before we're ready. But faith always requires us to do something. When we act on faith, we can be confident that God will be right there with us—helping carry the weight we are called to carry. Remember, you're carrying the yoke with Jesus, so you can trust that He's gonna pull what you can't. You stay focused on what you can do and trust that God will do what you can't do. When you do your best with what you have, you'll get a return on your work and you'll have something to give back to the Master.

What's kind of funny is, everything we're giving back to Him is His, anyway. But we get the joy of offering something to God. We aren't doing it to earn anything. We're doing it in gratitude, as a response to what He has already done for us that we didn't deserve. And we get the rewards of faithfulness just for doing something with what He gave us.

Make no mistake, just like those servants in the parable, God has given you some very specific talents and treasures. Typically, what He has given you is so natural to you that you think everyone has that gift—but they don't. Your gift is unique to you. Sometimes that gift brings lots of joy and confidence. Oftentimes, that gift can also feel like a burden. Our gifts and the unique burden we carry are typically connected. Even though it may feel like a burden, it's a gift.

When we use that gift and carry the burden that comes with it, knowing that burden is necessary suffering, we are being good stewards.

So let's look at how to use our talents and abilities wisely.

(Note: If you aren't convinced that you have a specific gift or aren't sure what it is, ask someone who knows you well. They do. Then believe them. Sometimes it's easier for others to identify our gift because we're just too close to it.)

Play to Your Strengths

I am mathematically challenged. The only math class in which I ever scored higher than a C was geometry, and that was with a lot of after-school tutoring. In college, I had to take algebra three times (the worst part was, it was from the same professor all those times ...)! Math and I are not friends. But when it came to writing and reading, I tended to make good grades with minimal effort. I often wonder how much more enjoyable school could have been if I never had to take a math course, but that's not the point of school: The goal of early education is to help us become well-rounded and learn to learn. If we're weak in one subject, we take extra classes and exert lots of effort to help us get stronger in that area.

There's value to being knowledgeable in all areas, but the fact is, in the real world outside of school, we hire people for different jobs because of their ability to specialize. We want someone who is laser-focused on what they're good at and have developed it to a high level. If I need heart surgery, I don't want a surgeon who splits his time between organic okra farming and operating on a human heart; I want someone who is totally focused on heart surgery, all the time!

It's good to try lots of stuff in school to figure out what you are and aren't good at. But at some point, we have to shift our mindset and realize that the best thing we can do is focus on improving what we're naturally good at doing. Too often, we get weighed down, trying to use brute force to work in areas that aren't ever going to be a strength for us. And it's exhausting!

Marcus Buckingham is a business consultant who talks about the importance of playing to your strengths. He points out that if you are a level five out of ten in a skill, you could work really hard and get your five up to a seven or eight at maximum. (I will never get higher than an eight in math, no matter how hard I try.) But if you're naturally an eight at something, there's a good chance that with focus and practice, you could become a ten.

I've always been drawn to writing and speaking. The more I do it, the clearer and sharper my skills become. I cringe when I read some of the stuff I wrote when I was just getting started. It was horrible. But I've gotten better over the years. But if I had spent loads of time getting better at math, rather than writing books, I would have limited my growth in the area of writing, because I only have so much time and energy. Any of it I give to math is taken from writing. It's unwise to spend lots of time and energy trying to improve on something you'll never be that great at. It's actually wasteful and doesn't tend to bring the returns the Master is looking for.

Wise stewardship focuses on improving what we have, not what we don't have.

This is really important, because in certain areas of life, there are roles and responsibilities God has given that only *you* can do well. You may not feel that gifted at it, but if God gave it to you, it means you can improve. In fact, you're *expected* to improve it.

Only you can be your child's parent.

Only you can be your spouse's partner.

If you're a business leader, pastor, or not-for-profit leader, only you can articulate and implement the unique vision for your church or organization.

Only you can care for your health.

You may not feel naturally gifted at being a parent or spouse, but if God gave you that role, He also gave you what you need to do it well. You may be in a leadership position you feel unqualified for, but if God gave you the position, trust that you have what you need.

If we don't fill these roles and responsibilities—or try to outsource them to teachers, the internet, or quick fixes—there's a good chance we'll only create more burdens for ourselves in the long run. And we won't like the results.

You have what you need right now to seek God's Kingdom in your specific gifting and calling. If God gave you the burden (a.k.a. the gift), you have the power you need right now to steward it well. Stay focused on doing what you can do. "His divine power has given us everything we need for a godly life through our knowledge of him who called us by his own glory and goodness."[8]

Half of staying focused is knowing what you've got. The other half is acknowledging what you don't have and what isn't the best use of your time, money, and energy. There are lots of things in life that have to be done, but not necessarily by you. In fact, some of those things *shouldn't* be done by you because they're taking time, money, or energy away from something that God says should be a priority.

Some of the things you dread doing and aren't that great at could be gladly taken on by someone who enjoys doing them—freeing up time for you to focus on what you're good at and only you can do. For example, I could do my taxes. (I used to, in fact—mostly because I was cheap and hardheaded about proving I could do it.) But I finally realized that the three days it takes me to work through it that I could be spending with my family, not to mention the frustration and potential mistakes it creates, just aren't worth it to me. I'd rather pay a few hundred dollars to let someone who actually enjoys doing taxes (and knows how to do them) take that job. And yes, there are people who actually enjoy doing tax returns and are good at it!

If you have the financial margin to pay someone, or there's someone around you who is better at something than you and enjoys it—maybe you should let them. If you can't afford to pay them, see if you can make a trade by helping them with something you are good at. You may need to turn the finances over to your spouse because, honestly, you're not good at it. You may need to delegate some things at work and release control—especially if taking on the project that isn't your gifting is going to create lots of anxiety and frustration and chaos in relationships that are a priority.

If it's not a role only you can fill or a job only you can do, give it to someone who enjoys doing that! Most importantly, figure out what only you can do, and make sure you're doing whatever it takes to give your best to that and build on what God has already given you. Because the truth is, typically, it's a very small amount of our focused effort that tends to yield the greatest results.

There's a really amazing principle God put into place that can help us establish how to get the most output from the least input. So let's look at how that principle applies to using your resources in a focused and intentional way for God's Kingdom.

The 80/20 Principle

In the late 1800s, a guy named Vilfredo Pareto noticed that about 20 percent of his pea plants were producing 80 percent of the peas in his garden. As an economist, he also noticed that 80 percent of the land in his home country of Italy was owned by about 20 percent of the population. He started exploring this 80/20 relationship and began to see it all over the place.

The Pareto Principle, or 80/20 Rule, states: For many outcomes, roughly 80 percent of consequences come from 20 percent of causes.[9] This insight can really be a game-changer in how you manage what God has given you. When you can identify the 20 percent of what you do that leads to the 80 percent in your life, it's makes it much easier to focus on the most productive tasks, because even little input in those areas leads to the greatest output.

When Emily told me I was working too much, I got really serious about focusing on what was bringing the greatest return on effort and offloading what wasn't. I used the 80/20 principle to look at my time, money, and energy (my treasure).

The tension point in my marriage was the amount of time

I was working. I knew the quickest way to lessen that tension was to completely stop working.

So I did.

Just kidding. But seriously, I knew I needed to provide for my family, so I started looking at the various parts of what I did that actually provided for us financially. Eighty percent of our income came from three sources: leadership coaching, speaking, and donations from ministry supporters.

As I delved a little deeper, I realized that what brought coaching clients, speaking gigs, and new ministry donors (my 80 percent) was one thing: content creation. Articles, books, and emails I wrote and the videos, radio shows, and podcasts I created or appeared in opened the door for speaking, coaching, and new ministry supporters. Creating content was the 20 percent that led to my 80 percent.

Next, I developed a plan for how to give my best time and energy to that 20 percent.

For most people (including me), the first three hours of their day after they wake up are their most productive in terms of energy and mental sharpness. So using those first three hours to maximum capacity is imperative. If you count the hours you're usually awake (sixteen, in theory), 20 percent of that is about three hours (three hours and twelve minutes, to be exact). So, as best as I can, I make sure those three hours are focused on creating content and writing.

Interestingly, I also found that when I dedicated at least twenty minutes of those first three hours to reading my Bible, praying, and preparing for the day, it really set me in a good mental and spiritual place. (Hmm . . . twenty minutes is roughly 10 percent of those first three hours, like a tithe . . . coincidence?)

I save administrative work for the afternoon, when I don't have to be as mentally sharp; most of my administrative tasks are routine. And whenever I can, I just outsource them to someone who actually gets a kick out of doing that stuff.

The amount of time and structure this little principle has given me has changed my life. When I stick with it, I get a lot done and have time, money, and energy to give my best to those who deserve it most in my life. When I don't, the weight of work and life balance gets heavy.

If you want to really lighten your load, it's really, really important to take some time to evaluate what the 20 percent is that brings your 80 percent, in all areas of your life. Figure out what you can focus on that brings the greatest results.

Working harder will just wear you out. Working smarter and using wisdom will help you increase what God has given you.

Again, finding what's most important is a moving target that requires regular evaluation in each season. But when you understand how the Pareto principle applies to your situation, it can change everything. Here are a few areas that can easily get out of balance in life where I've found the 80/20 rule to be particularly helpful.

80/20 Marriage and Relationships

Relationships require effort, so figuring out how to invest in yours in the way that has the most impact can go a long way. In *The Five Love Languages*, Gary Chapman talks about the five ways we fill our "love tank": words of affirmation, quality time, giving and receiving gifts, physical affection, and acts of service. When you know what love language best fills the tank of those around you, it's a helpful cue for where to give your best 20 percent.

My wife's love language is quality time—which means I need to devote large amounts of time to undistracted listening and gazing into her eyes. If I'm distracted, it doesn't count. So quality time typically isn't possible when our daughter is around because she distracts our attention. Also, if I'm tired, things aren't gonna go well. So I have to make sure I create intentional space to give Emily undistracted time when I have energy. When I do this, even in small amounts, I like the results!

My love language is words of affirmation. Emily's got it easy. Just a few words of encouragement from her can keep me going for days.

Figure out what investment of yourself brings the greatest sense of connection and fulfillment in your marriage and relationships, then focus on giving your best time, money, and energy to that. A little bit can go a long way if you're focused on the right thing.

Important note: There is no trade-off for presence, proximity, and unhurried time in relationships. Healthy relationships require an investment of love and guidance from the Holy Spirit. In some seasons, you'll need to focus way more energy on certain relationships than others. So don't fall into the trap of thinking this 80/20 thing is a cure-all or a box you can check that will make all your relationships healthy while you go on your merry way doing whatever you want. The 80/20 rule is more a guiding principle to help you evaluate whether you're giving your most important relationships your best focus.

80/20 Parenting

What's the 20 percent that yields the greatest results in your relationship with your child(ren)? I know, kids can be a sucking vortex of need, and when you give a little, they just want more, more, more. (*Do it again, Dad, again!*) But there's typically something you do with your kids that really resonates with them. Is it conversation? Is it doing activities together? Much of it depends on your child's personality. If they're talkative, you'll probably find that just listening to them is the 20 percent. If they're more tactile, your best bet might be building or creating things with them.

My daughter is eight. In her current season, wrestling seems to be what makes her feel most connected to me. Every afternoon she begs me to wrestle with her. I let her win most of the time, but she seems to enjoy the struggle of me pinning her down and her struggling to break free. It's exhausting for me, especially the stronger and more skilled she gets, but this effort brings a sense of closeness in our relationship. Typically, she gets worn out after a few minutes and wanders off to do something else, but the time fills her love tank.

Again, this changes in each season. I know one day she'll be an emotional teenager and I'll long for the simpler days when letting her put me in a choke hold did the trick!

80/20 Leadership

Leaders have to wear lots of hats, so getting this 80/20 thing right is really important. As leaders' responsibilities grow, we have to adapt our 80/20 accordingly. I've talked to leaders who realized that, in the early days, they used to spend their 20 percent doing the work (manual labor, hospital visits, direct interaction with people), but as responsibilities expanded, they had to shift their 20 percent energy to mentoring and training others to do those tasks for them. The time they normally spent interacting directly with customers, employees, or congregants instead became the time poured into raising up and empowering young leaders who took over in those roles.

This was a hard transition for many. In fact, some decided not to do it. Some couldn't release the direct interaction because they were insecure—feeling they needed to be the only one in that role and have total control. Others decided not to shift because they realized they really didn't *want* their church or business to grow any more. They felt so passionate about being directly connected with the people they served that they chose not to raise up others. And that's perfectly fine, if that's really your motive. The important thing is that it was an intentional decision, so they weren't frustrated by limited growth. It was a conscious sacrifice they had made to live by their values.

Only you can decide—through prayer and seeking counsel—what your role as a leader will require in this season. If you feel God calling you to be the main person in leadership, wearing all the hats, that's your decision; just know that the cost will be twofold. Unless you keep strict boundaries, you'll probably find yourself exhausted, trying to carry everything. Secondly, there's a chance that the work won't last beyond your life. (Which is fine; we aren't here to build our kingdom, we're here to build God's Kingdom.)

But I've also talked to lots of leaders who are frustrated that there are no other leaders in their organization to carry on their work. Typically, that's because those other leaders were never given the opportunities to step up because the main leader had decided they wanted to give their 20 percent not to mentoring others but to doing the work themselves. (And, of course, sometimes it's just because the leader is too insecure to give away any authority.) Again, there's nothing wrong with this, but just know it will cost you other leaders to carry on the work.

Can you imagine what kind of freedom and space you could create in your time, money, and energy if you got serious about stewarding your family, finances, and career? Based on personal experience, it's worth your time to figure out what your 20 percent is that leads to the eighty. Again, there needs to be a hierarchy and order. You may need to sacrifice some things in this season to give your best to the twenty that creates the eighty. That's wise stewardship.

You may feel overwhelmed and limited, but take heart. You are already uniquely equipped to accomplish God's purposes in your life. Stay focused on what you are gifted to do, and do it to the best of your ability. Use what God has given you, no matter how little or insignificant it may seem, the best you can. As you stay focused, you can be confident He'll give you what your heart really desires. Bring others in to do what you can't, and give them room to pursue the dreams God has placed in them. But above all, stay in lockstep with Jesus—one step at a time—as you share the yoke of the burden together. Carry what is yours to carry. No more, no less.

Next, let's look at how to figure out exactly what is yours to carry right now and what isn't. There's a good chance you're carrying some things that don't belong in your pack, and leaving those things behind could give you some new-found freedom.

4

Responsibility

The price of greatness is responsibility.

—Winston Churchill

A few years ago, when I was dealing with some major disappointment and frustration about the direction of my life, a guy recommended I hire a really expensive coach to help me through it. I was hesitant. Honestly, I thought *What could he possibly know that I don't already know?*

My friend told me, "Do one session. Do everything he says. If something good doesn't come of it, don't do it anymore."

That first session, the coach told me, "The only thing holding you back right now is your mindset."

I thought that was ridiculous. Among other things, lack of money and connections were holding me back. But over the next few weeks, I started to unpack how I saw the world. I realized I really did have some bad mindsets. That was when things started to change.

Here's what I realized in that season of self-discovery:

1. Whenever I don't like something about my life, I have to assume I am the problem—not the world. There is something I don't understand, either about myself or how people work, so I start reading, praying, and asking questions. I seek out advice, then shut up and listen to what people say; I don't make excuses for why my situation is special. It's not.

2. I am not special, and no one is going to "discover" me and launch me to success. The cavalry isn't coming to save me. I have what I need right now to build what I need right now. Big success builds on small success. But *I* must build and stop waiting for some magic moment or person to propel me forward. God will honor work that starts small and builds slowly.

3. I think I am so talented and amazing, but I'm not. I am mediocre at best. But I can get better with thousands and thousands of hours of disciplined practice. But no matter how good I might get, I always remember the words of Rochefoucauld: "The art of using moderate abilities to advantage often brings greater results than actual brilliance."[1]

4. No one owes me anything. God will provide for me, but He'll do it through my hard work—using the talents and skills He gave me and the ones I'll acquire as I continue to learn and grow.

5. There are no overnight success stories. All true success (anything on social media is not real success) has a backstory of work and sacrifice. If I want success, I need to think in terms of decades, not weeks or days. Success is a direction, not a destination. I can be successful the moment I start moving in the right direction.

It hurt to admit a few of those things. But as I look back at many of those realizations, I see I had to be willing to see myself as someone capable of doing whatever it took to get where I wanted to go. I had to take responsibility for what was mine to carry and trust God to carry what only He could carry.

Much of that mindset the coach was talking about came down to my willingness to change how I saw the obstacles I faced and embrace the power God had already given me to confront them. It was my responsibility to face my unique challenges with the unique tools God had already given me.

I'm guessing there are a handful of things in your life that have you frustrated or discouraged right now. I'm guessing you have some relationships that leave you feeling over-whelmed and confused—unsure of what you can do to fix them. Or maybe you're doing your best to provide for your family, but you just can't seem to get ahead. And it's exhausting. You really want to believe God will provide, but by all indications, if you don't keep up your current pace, your family will be in serious need.

When Jesus said, "Take my yoke upon you . . . For my yoke is easy and my burden is light,"[2] He was saying we all have a level of responsibility to carry. We all have something we have to carry. But when we're seeking God's Kingdom, that burden should be manageable because Jesus shares the weight. If the burden of life is feeling too heavy, we need to really slow down and figure out why.

We must constantly wrestle with the question: *How much of what I'm struggling with is mine to carry?* You can't take too much responsibility for what is truly your responsibility. But taking responsibility for what isn't your responsibility leads to frustration and feeling overwhelmed.

When we commit to finding a balance through constant adjustment and self-awareness of our motivations, it brings peace and confidence in our lives and the lives of those around us. So let's look at exactly how to do that: find balance.

The Responsibility Connection

I spoke to a group of pastors recently, and afterward, one of them told me that he realized he was angry with his congregation and staff. The resentment had been building for years. Later that afternoon, we talked it through, trying to figure out *why* he was frustrated. During the course of the conversation, it became pretty clear that the congregation and staff were actually looking for him to be more assertive.

I asked, "When are you gonna move them forward? They seem frustrated that you aren't leading."

He admitted, "I've been afraid to lead them. They fired the last pastor who made changes in the church." (Unfortunately, I hear this from a lot of pastors.)

I asked how long he had been serving at the church. I was shocked when he said, "Twelve years." It was no wonder frustration was building between him and the congregation. He had put in more than enough time to build the trust he needed to lead, but he was afraid to step up and take on his role as leader.

There's a connection between frustration and responsibility. When we're responsible for something and don't step up, it creates frustration in us and those around us.

I know lots of parents who are frustrated and resentful about how their young children are behaving. In many of those cases, those parents have abdicated their responsibility to slow down and take the time to lovingly discipline their kids. One parent told me, "I'm afraid if I'm too hard on them, they won't love me, or they'll rebel." The sad truth is, when we don't take responsibility for raising our kids, someone else will—and it probably won't be the people we'd choose. Culture, TV, and the government don't truly love your children. But you do, which is why getting responsibility right is so important.

If we don't take responsibility (a form of stewardship) for what is ours to care for, we may find ourselves getting frustrated at who, or what, steps up to fill the void.

David, a fearless shepherd boy, wasn't afraid to face the giant Goliath. But the reason he had to step up was that Saul, the king and commander of the army, was afraid to attack the giant who was threatening Israel. Saul had the armor and the authority, but he didn't take action. So instead, David killed Goliath and led the entire army to victory. He became a hero overnight, and people started singing his praises. Sadly, Saul saw this and viewed David as an enemy for the rest of his life.[3] But all David did was step up when no one else would. We can't afford to check out when responsibility is calling on us to lead.

I've seen lots of burnt-out, or just bored, leaders who find a project that excites them—a new business prospect or international mission. They aren't willing to step out and go full-time at the new venture because they need their stable income, but they end up neglecting their businesses or churches to pursue those new opportunities because that's where their heart is. Usually, the strongest person still at the organization ends up seizing control, either in a power grab or because they're just trying to keep it afloat. But those people who fill in the gap aren't ultimately responsible for the organization, so it creates frustration and stress among the staff. The best staff members quit and lots of people are left disillusioned, all because the leader isn't willing to exert the energy to take responsibility for what they've been given.

The same thing happens when tired or distracted parents turn their kids over to TV, teachers, or other adults, or when they mentally check out by scrolling through social media. The results are always negative in the long run. That's why it's so important to constantly evaluate our level of responsibility in every situation. If we're faced with a major challenge, rather than run and hide or helplessly throw our hands up in the air, we need to simply slow down and look at the problem. We typically have more ability to change a situation in our personal lives than we realize, if we'll properly evaluate it.

A Swarm of Locus

About a year after we got married, Emily and I moved to southern Mexico to run a retreat center. I thought we were going there to teach and minister to locals, but in reality, it was because I was about to get schooled in all sorts of character development. We were right on the Pacific Ocean, and much of my job consisted of fixing anything the salty air had destroyed. Light fixtures, water pumps, air conditioners, you name it—everything was constantly rotting. I sprayed things down with fresh water and coated them with oil, but that only slowed the decay. Something major broke literally every week. I lived in a constant state of frustration and worry, always wondering what was going to break next.

Up to that point in my life, if something broke, I'd just throw my hands up and call a repairman (then get irritated about how much he charged) or buy a replacement. I didn't even bother trying to fix things. But my experience in Mexico was about to pull out a side of me I didn't even know was there.

Within three days of our arrival, the first challenge came. The freezer we'd inherited from the previous missionaries broke. I called the guy who had lived there before us and asked him who I should call to fix it.

He laughed. "You have to do it. Nobody will come out there."

So I laughed back, "Bro, I am not mechanically inclined."

"Well, you're gonna have to learn," he said. "Just take twenty minutes to really look at it. Look for what seems off."

I didn't want to look at it; I just wanted it fixed. We were there to minister to people, not fix broken stuff!

After some pouting, I finally surrendered to the fact that I was the one responsible for fixing the fridge. It would not fix itself. Since I had no idea what I was doing, I called my Mexican friend, Max. He came over, grabbed a screwdriver, and just started taking the freezer apart.

I was a bit concerned. "Have you ever done this before?"

He smiled. "No. But we'll figure it out. We just have to look for what looks wrong."

We popped off a few panels and quickly saw it. A "thingy" was cracked and frozen over. We took the "thingy" to a store and said, "*Necesitamos esto.*" ("We need one of these.") We paid a few bucks, took the part home, replaced it, and *voila!* I had fixed a freezer. (Sort of; Max actually did). But I felt I was back in control of my life.

Over the next six months, I fixed two water pumps, an air conditioner, a water heater, a pool pump, a sewer system, a roof, and several other random things on my own. Each time, I had to remind myself to slow down, really look at the problem, and take whatever small steps I could to resolve the issue. I found I was much more capable of fixing things than I had previously believed. I think that process applies to pretty much any challenge we face in life.

If God has given you a burden to carry, He has also given you what you need to carry that burden, with His help. We just need to step up and take responsibility in that situation.

In every challenge we face, we land somewhere on a continuum between taking total responsibility (even if it's not *all* our responsibility) and taking no responsibility. We tend to make decisions about this level of responsibility based on what psychologists call our locus of control.

Our locus of control has two extremes: external and internal.

External Locus of Control	Internal Locus of Control
I'm helpless to do anything about this; other people are responsible for my situation.	I'm responsible, my actions make a difference, and I can change things.

Interestingly, the two extremes of mental illness—neuroses and character disorders—tend to fall on one extreme or the other of that continuum as well. A neurosis is taking total responsibility for everything that happens, even if it's not your fault. (I tend to be mildly neurotic most of the time.) A character disorder is not taking any responsibility, even when there's something you can do to change the situation.

The research is pretty clear that people with an internal locus of control are less likely to be overweight, more likely to describe themselves as healthy, and show lower levels of psychological stress. A balanced, internal locus of control is the key to living well.

We're complex, so we can have an internal locus of control in one situation and an external locus of control in another situation, at the same time. When life is hard and we're pedaling as fast as we can to keep up, it's easy to lean toward one of the extremes. You may confidently lead a small army of people at work but feel helpless against the three-year-old tyrant in your home who refuses to take a bath. I've met brilliant women and men, people at the top of their fields in business and ministry, who feel helpless to solve problems in their personal lives.

Feeling helpless actually impairs something called executive function: We freeze up and lose our ability to perform tasks we're perfectly capable of performing. While I was rafting the Grand Canyon a few years ago, the guide said, "When you're on the river, you must become an active participant in your own survival." He said when people fell out of the raft, they'd panic and lose their capacity to think. He said the team would actively try to rescue anyone who fell out, but we had to swim hard toward the raft and play a part in the rescue.

I think that advice also applies when the rapids of life get wild: As best as you can, become an active participant in your own survival. You are way more capable than you may give yourself credit for.

Remember,

> If the Spirit of him who raised Jesus from the dead dwells in you, he who raised Christ Jesus from the dead will also give life to your mortal bodies through his Spirit who dwells in you.[4]

The strength you need to live the life God has called you

to comes from Him. Using brute force or willpower will only lead to more exhaustion. Sharing the load with Him will bring peace and strength.

Here's a sobering truth: We tend to have more control than we believe we do—but fear can cause us to shrink back. It's a whole lot easier to blame something or someone for our situation. But blaming and feeling like a victim only lead to resentment. Taking on more than what is yours to carry will do the same.

So let's look at how to find a balance of what to carry and what to leave behind.

Finding the Balance

I heard a story once about a guy who was working hard in the heat, pulling weeds out of his garden. A neighbor walked by and said, "Wow! What a beautiful garden God has given you!"

The man looked up, sweat pouring down his face, and grunted, "Yeah? Well, you should have seen all the weeds in God's garden before I got involved!"

One of the great challenges in seeking God's Kingdom is

realizing that faith is a balance of trusting God and working your tail off. Trusting God and working hard aren't mutually exclusive. In fact, living a life of faith requires work. "Faith by itself, if it does not have works, is dead."[5] As Irenaeus said, "Work as if it depends on you and pray as if it depends on God." Both are true. We do our part and trust God to do His.

And this is where it gets tricky.

If you're reading this book, I'd be willing to bet you err on the side of working too hard. People who read books about priorities tend to be responsible people. But often, we're over-responsible because we believe it's ultimately on us. But we were never made to carry the weight of the world; Jesus already did.

A dear friend of mine who was in college was constantly stressing about her grades. It was causing her major anxiety. She would study late into the night, rarely getting sleep. The crazy thing is, she always made A's. In fact, her GPA was higher than a 4.0. I told her once, "The highest grade you can make is an A. Figure out how much work it takes to get an A—then only do that much. Save your energy for other stuff."

Her response was telling. "Yeah, but what if one of the tests is harder than all the rest and I end up failing?"

Now, I seriously doubt she would have failed. But I think that statement explains a lot of the anxiety many of us feel. We've all had experiences that didn't go well and, if we look back honestly, we wonder if it was because we didn't put in enough effort. A responsible person will naturally work harder to make sure that never happens again.

As someone who is constantly wondering if I should do more, here's what I've concluded: If, to the best of our knowledge and ability, we've done what we could, then we have to leave the results to God. If we experience what we feel is lack after having taken responsibility, then we can be at peace and trust that His grace is sufficient in this season. We have what we need for right now.

Do I like that conclusion? No. But that's where we have to find peace in what Paul says: "Godliness with contentment is great gain."[6] When we trust that we did our best and believe that what God brings from that work is enough—even if it feels like it's not—we show faith. And faith pleases God.

Am I saying to just accept all struggle and lack as God's will? No way! I'm saying that if you've done everything you can do to take responsibility for what God has given you, and the situation just isn't what you want, learn to be content and work within the limitations in front of you. In the words of

T. S. Eliot: "When forced to work within a strict framework, the imagination is taxed to its utmost and will produce its richest ideas. Given total freedom, the work is likely to sprawl."[7] Which is basically what Paul heard from God when he was facing his own limits: "My grace is sufficient for you, for my power is made perfect in weakness."[8] Typically, it's when our limitation is abundantly clear that God does His greatest work in our lives.

Slow Down and Look at It

When something would break on that property in Mexico, I regularly had to remind myself what David had said: "Just take twenty minutes to look at it carefully." The same is true in life when we face any challenge relationally, emotionally, or physically. Really evaluate. Look from multiple angles. If it's a really complex problem, seek outside help. Figure out what you can—and can't—do to resolve the situation.

It's the classic prayer of Reinhold Niebuhr: "God grant me the serenity to accept the things I cannot change, courage to change the things I can, and wisdom to know the difference."[9]

You may be in a situation where things seem so out of

control that you feel absolutely helpless in the face of the challenges. If you're there, here's my advice: aim lower.

You always have the power to change *some*thing. It may be as simple as your attitude. You may never be able to change your boss or your ex, but you can change your attitude. And you are the only one who can change your attitude. It may seem tiny or insignificant in the face of an even bigger problem, but don't worry about the bigger problem—do what you can do. When you take responsibility for what you can change—stop ignoring bad behavior, stop checking out, lovingly and wisely discipline the kids—it's pretty common for other things to start to change.

Take an honest look at your life right now. What's bothering you? Is it within your control? What are you responsible for that, with a little work, you could actually change right now? Are you willing to do the work to change it?

There's a good chance there's something you can change that you've been afraid to take responsibility for. Afraid of the work involved. Afraid you might fail. Is it possible that avoiding taking responsibility is actually creating more burden (emotionally, physically, relationally) than just dealing with the issue? If you've been running from responsibility, please, please, please go face it! Have the conversation. Fill out the paperwork. Look at the debt balance. Just face it. Don't back down. Blaming is easy, but it only leads to victim-hood and anger.

You can't fix everything, but you can fix some things. You are far more capable than you give yourself credit for. God can give you the strength to do what you need to do. The best news is that if you'll do your part, God will come in and do what you can't do on your own. And every small step you take to lighten the load of what you shouldn't be carrying makes things, well, lighter.

When you properly evaluate what's yours to carry and what isn't, you tend to find there's actually more freedom in your life than you may have thought. When you do what needs to be done, it tends to open up lots of possibilities and freedom. So let's talk about that next: the freedom of margin.

5

Margin

God is always trying to give good things to us,
but our hands are too full to receive them.

—*St. Augustine*

When I was a kid, I entered the home of a distant aunt of mine after she passed away. She was a hoarder. Every nook and cranny of the house was packed with stuff. It was piled so high with magazines, cat food, and boxes that all the windows were blocked and light couldn't even get in. It was a pretty dark place until we started pulling things out.

I love Proverbs 4:18: "The path of the righteous is like the light of dawn, which shines brighter and brighter until full day." God promises a bright future for those seeking His Kingdom, but oftentimes we pile things so high in our lives that the light can't get in. Even good things can fill our lives to the point that we feel cramped, with no space, time, or energy.

It's been said that God is always trying to give good things to us, but our hands are too full to receive them.[1] It's like when you go on vacation with a full suitcase, then find that perfect souvenir but have no space to bring it back with you. You think, *How am I gonna fit that in?* You have to choose between either not getting the cool souvenir, leaving something behind, or buying a bigger bag.

I'm pretty certain that right now, you've got some situations or challenges that leave you saying: "How am I gonna fit that in?" For some personality types, that question is an exciting challenge. You're certain there's always one more thing you can cram in by the sheer exertion of your will. You just *know* you can fit it in somewhere. But periodically, you find yourself crashing under the weight of everything you've crammed into your bag.

For the rest of us, when a new challenge or situation arises that will require our time, money, or energy, we ask that question with a sense of dread. We know tension is building with our spouse and we need to talk, but we just don't have the emotional energy or time for a heated two-hour conversation. We know we need to get more serious about changing a habit, but there's just no space for it. I regularly work with people who want a more fulfilling job, but they can't afford to take one that pays less because their mortgage and debt load is based on their current level of income. As life happens, the commitment of our time, money, and energy gets so full that we have no room for more.

And it can feel oppressive. Like you're trapped in a crowded house.

I am sure that distant relative of mine really thought she needed all that stuff she was hoarding. It brought her a sense of security or connection. But ultimately, she became a slave to protecting it.

That is the nature of adding stuff. Adding more requires more. When you get a nicer car, your insurance goes up. You get a new house, and it comes with all sorts of extra expenses you never expected. Before you know it, what you own owns you.

There's a word we have for situations in which a person is owned or oppressed by outside forces:

Slave (n): a person who is completely subservient to a dominating influence.[2]

A slave is someone who has no say over their lives and how they use their time, money, and energy. I think we can all relate to feeling like slaves at times. And know this: Without intentionality, we will always fall into slavery. Freedom isn't our default setting.

That's why the Apostle Paul reminds us: "It is for freedom that Christ has set us free. Stand firm, then, and do not let yourselves be burdened again by a yoke of slavery."[3] Jesus came to set us free from slavery to sin and values that are out of line with God's Kingdom. We're free, but it's a unique freedom. Because the fact is, we're naturally going to serve something. It's in our nature. But we can choose what enslaves us. When we're a slave to the *right* thing, it actually brings freedom. That's what Paul is talking about when he says,

> But thanks be to God that, though you used to be slaves to sin, you have come to obey from your heart the pattern of teaching that has now claimed your allegiance. You have been set free from sin and have become slaves to righteousness.[4]

When we choose to be controlled by seeking God's Kingdom and righteousness, we find freedom. But walking in freedom is an ongoing decision that requires vigilance. We're always prone to fill every space in our lives and become slaves to lesser things again. Sometimes we fill gaps out of fear. Sometimes it's because we feel a need to prove ourselves and want to justify our existence on the planet by staying busy. Sometimes it's just because we want to soak up every last drop of life—bigger, better, faster! But when we have no margin or space, it quickly leads to us feeling enslaved and overwhelmed—trapped in our jobs, trapped in obligations, trapped in debt.

Fortunately, there's a path to freedom.

One of the most faith-filled decisions we can make is to intentionally create margin in our lives. Margin in our finances. Margin in our energy. Margin in our time. Choosing not to overload our finances, energy, and time is essentially an act of faith, saying, "I know there's so much good out there that I'm going to leave space for it when it gets here."

There are lots of areas in our lives where margin is important, but I want to focus on one specific area where having more margin in your life can create a new level of freedom. If you can get some space here, it tends to open doors to space in lots of other areas. Read on.

Your Greatest Asset

I took a group of high net-worth individuals hiking a while back. About three days into our trip, I had a realization: *These people think very differently than I do.*

They thought about pretty much everything differently—particularly money.

I shared the observation with one of the guys on the trip. He told me something that has stuck with me: "Yeah. Once you make a bunch of money, you look around and realize that the most valuable thing isn't money, it's time. They aren't making more of it."

That statement really shifted my perspective. I don't know about you, but I spend about twenty-two hours of the day concerned about money. *Will I be able to provide for my family? What if we can't cover the bills one month?* I give a lot of value to money and what I think it can give me. It's a highly limited resource in my mind. But you can always make more money. And you can always get more energy—just chug some coffee! But once a specific space in time is gone, it's gone, man! Which is what King David was talking about when he said, "So teach us to number our days that we may get a heart of wisdom."[5] A wise person values time.

I'm no millionaire, but that conversation got me thinking: What would it look like if I started valuing time as my most important resource? What if my time was more valuable than money or energy? When you think in those terms, the question then becomes: *What am I doing with my time?*

When my daughter was born, I woke up to the reality of just how much time I used to have. What had I done with it? I could've written, like, twenty books! When I look at my time honestly, I realize that I don't always use it in the best way. I spend ridiculous amounts of time scrolling through social media. There's nothing wrong with relaxing, but really, that isn't even that relaxing. It doesn't leave me feeling truly rejuvenated like other things do; it's just convenient and always available. I spend all that time on social media and then feel like I don't have time to get important stuff done. The fact is, I have the time, but I don't prioritize using it well.

Time is your most important asset. Period.

Time is a lot of what we're giving to our employers. Sure, you're giving knowledge and skill, but it takes your time. Even if you aren't paid hourly, typically a big part of what your employer is paying for is access to your time. (Which is why I've talked to lots of people who realized the first step to starting their own side hustle that ultimately led to more income was to focus on getting more time on their terms, while balancing keeping their day job.) When we have control of our time, it tends to lead to more control over our money and energy.

I've found that the people I see as most successful actually tend to have lots of free space in their calendar. Yes, they have huge responsibility and influence, but they aren't tyrannized by their schedules. They guard their time carefully and dictate their schedule. They aren't constantly giving their time to what seems urgent. (And something always seems urgent!)

Dave Ramsey often points out that when you have an emergency fund of a thousand dollars set aside (financial margin), there are a lot fewer situations that feel like emergencies. I've found the same is true with time. As I've incorporated the practice of having more margin in my life (an emergency time fund, so to speak), fewer things seem urgent or pressing. And when something truly urgent does come up, I have the resources to deal with it; it doesn't become an oppressive weight or throw my schedule into disarray. More margin in our time creates more peace and more opportunities.

An increasing amount of evidence shows that more time and space leads to greater creativity and better problem-solving skills. Teresa Amabile, a Harvard researcher, found that people under high levels of time pressure are 45 percent less likely to come up with creative solutions because they're constantly operating under something she calls "pressure hangover."[6] Scott Barry Kaufman conducted several surveys and found that 72 percent of people have their best ideas in the shower.[7] Why? Because they were relaxed and not under pressure.

I think that's why God asks us to take a mandatory break once per week. He asks us to stop working, stop trying to provide, and just chill out and leave some space. When we seek His Kingdom by honoring a sabbath day of rest, we can be sure that it will take weight off our shoulders.

A Day-Long Breath

I lead a hike through Israel where we walk where Jesus spent most of His time. Over five days, we hike from Nazareth to the Mount of Beatitudes. We stop in Cana—where Jesus did His first miracle—then head up Mount Arbel, over the Horns of Hattin—the site of a famous Crusade battle—and down to Magdala and Capernaum on the shores of Galilee. On our final night, we stay at the convent on the Mount of Beatitudes.

The first time I did that hike, when I was booking the accommodations, I ran into a roadblock I hadn't anticipated. One of our overnight stops was scheduled to take place at an Orthodox Jewish kibbutz, a collective farm. Orthodox Jews won't take guests from Friday night to Saturday night because that twenty-four-hour period is their sacred Shabbat, a Sabbath day of rest. They are strict about it. So strict, in fact, that I had to rearrange our entire schedule around it.

Most of Israel, particularly Jerusalem, completely shuts down on Shabbat. All but a handful of restaurants and stores close. They take it so seriously that most buildings there are equipped with Shabbat elevators: the buttons are disabled so you don't "work" by pushing them. Instead, the elevator stops at each floor, opens, then closes. If you're staying on the

thirtieth floor and accidentally end up on one of these elevators, you'd better get comfortable, because it's gonna be a
long ride. Some hotels won't even let you use their coffee
makers on Shabbat. (Talk about a tension point!) They take
rest seriously, because . . . rest is a serious thing. In fact, God
didn't just suggest a day of rest, He actually commanded it.
And He gave a really good reason for it.

> "The seventh day is a sabbath to the LORD your
> God. On it you shall not do any work. . . .
> Remember that you were slaves in Egypt and that
> the Lord your God brought you out of there with
> a mighty hand and an outstretched arm. Therefore
> the Lord your God has commanded you to observe
> the Sabbath day."[8]

Taking a day of rest is a weekly reminder that we aren't
slaves. Only free people can take an entire day to rest from
the demands of life. God is serious about keeping us out of
slavery.

We're made to work and create. Working hard is a good
thing. But we should be just as intentional about resting hard.

Rest builds strength. If you've ever taken on a strict exercise regimen, you know a good trainer will make you take rest days for your muscles to recover. Recovering is as important as pushing. When we don't take time to rest, it can have horrible consequences. As productivity increases around the world, we are seeing the harmful effects of too much work. In fact, for a while, Japan experienced an epidemic of people dying from something they called *karoshi*—that is, working to death.[9] When life is all work and no rest, you can be certain that at some point, things are going to turn ugly.

Genesis tells us God spent six days working and then He rested. The Psalms seem to indicate that God never sleeps, so I doubt He actually slept—but you can be certain it was a time that God kicked back, took a deep breath, and enjoyed what he had created. We need time to enjoy the fruits of our labor, too. We need time to relax and process the results of our work.

Making a lot of strict rules about not working leads to legalism and more slavery, so that's not the goal here. But it is wise to set some parameters for what our rest day will look like. A Sabbath day shouldn't be a time to catch up on all the stuff you didn't get done during the week. That defeats the whole purpose! Taking a Sabbath may mean things are left undone. Some laundry may be left unfolded for a day. The home project may not get done this week. Cut yourself some slack. Don't worry. You're resourceful; you'll get that other stuff done eventually. But you'll get it done even faster and better if you're rested when you do it.

You may work on the weekends (like me), so the traditional rest days of Saturday or Sunday may not work for you. But you can choose any day. Just establish a plan beforehand for how you'll give yourself time to just breathe. Prep your meals the night before. Use a slow cooker. Turn off your phone. Don't schedule anything but family time on those days.

Sabbath is an act of faith. It's giving God a focused day of our lives and trusting that He will keep things running while you take a breather. (Of course, He's always keeping things running . . . maybe we should breathe a lot more easily all of the time.) God valued a day of rest, and so should we. Sabbath reminds us that God is on the throne and in His place—which helps remind us that He wants us to carry only what He asked us to carry and trust Him to help us carry what we can't on our own.

If you're going to keep it light in your life, you'll need to prioritize a rhythm of weekly rest through Sabbath—a specific day each week when you stop doing what you're doing, set the pack of your burden down, and trust that God will keep the world running while you rest.

I understand that if you've felt like a slave to time, making space can be really hard. So let's talk about how to do that.

Stopping Isn't Failure

In the early days of the COVID-19 pandemic, before people knew what we were dealing with, the world came to a screeching halt. Our church was closed for a few Sundays and, even after we reopened, attendance was low. For obvious reasons, we ended up cutting back on lots of things we used to offer because the demand and volunteers just weren't there anymore. I asked our senior pastor if he was frustrated about it all. His response surprised me. He said he was actually grateful for the reset.

He said there were lots of things he realized the church was doing that weren't really necessary or serving the overall mission of what a church is about. Some were things that had long outlived their purpose, but no one had the courage to curtail. He decided to be very strategic about rebooting only what served the key purposes of outreach and ministry for the church. At first he was worried that people would be upset about him not restarting certain ministries—but no one said anything! The best part was, it freed up volunteers, finances, and time for the most important ministries of the church.

I think the same is true in our lives. From time to time, we need to stop, look around, and figure out if there's something we just need to stop doing. We need to look at the season and see if there's anything that isn't serving our current priorities. If so, stop doing those things!

Stopping isn't failure. Some things need to end. There's no shame in stopping something that isn't serving its intended purpose. In fact, it actually shows you're mentally healthy. It's been said that the definition of insanity is doing the same thing over and over and expecting different results. If something isn't serving the overall goals you have for yourself and your family, stop doing it!

Sometimes this means making drastic changes. You may need to start looking for another job. You may need to drive a cheaper car or live in a smaller house because the stress is just getting to be too much. Don't lose your family and peace and joy over a house, or a job, or a paycheck.

But more often than not, for most of us, this just requires a few tweaks. We need to say no to a few good things to make room for the best things. Golf may need to be set aside for a season so you can spend Saturday mornings with your young kids. You may need to back off on volunteering at a few places to give time to your family. It won't be forever, but it's important now.

What could your life look like if you had a little more space in your time, money, and energy? Get serious about giving yourself some breathing room in those areas. Drop an activity or two. Buy a house or car that is less than what you can afford so you'll have money to be generous or travel. Schedule fewer meetings, but give the people you do meet with lots more time and attention. Speaking of that, let's talk briefly about the importance of margin in communication.

Communication Requires Margin

I was in the kitchen recently when my wife rounded the corner and saw me spreading mayonnaise on some bread.

"What are you doing?" she asked.

"Making a sandwich."

"Can't you just go somewhere else?"

I looked around. "Uh, no. I'm making lunch. Where you make lunch—in the kitchen."

The conversation escalated from there but I'll leave out the details so you'll think my marriage is great. But, apparently, my very presence at home was a problem. I'm not the sharpest tool in the shed, but I've come to realize that when me just being in the house irritates my wife, it's a sign that tension has been building in our relationship and we need to talk.

After a few minutes of sallying back and forth, with me completely baffled about what I had done wrong by making a sandwich, it all came out. Emily said: "Yesterday, when you _____, I felt like you didn't care about me. But I didn't realize it until just now."

Here's an important truth I've learned: Most of us don't know what we're feeling or thinking until we're given the time to talk it out. We're all just moving ahead, trying to live our lives. We're typically so busy that there's no time to really work through things—so we just press ahead, and tension builds. We know our spending is out of control, but there's not time to sit down and figure out why. We know that we are running around like chickens with our heads cut off trying to keep up with schedules, but there's no time to evaluate what's actually causing the stress.

Because most of us don't know what's really going on inside of us until we say it out loud, we need unhurried time—margin—to communicate and process it. We clarify what we think and feel by speaking, which is why one of the greatest gifts you can give to yourself and others is time and space to express yourself freely. (It's also why freedom of speech is so important.) Whether we do it with other people, with God, or even by journaling by ourselves, we think by communicating.

Marriage experts say that we need at least ninety minutes per week just to communicate with our families about schedules and responsibilities that need our attention—sports schedules, bills to be paid, future plans. And that's just to talk about the facts and details. If you really want emotional connection, you'll need more time than that. That's why date nights are important if you're married. And I'm talking about date nights that don't involve watching a movie or zoning out.

You need dedicated time to communicate and connect emotionally—to figure out what you're really feeling.

That's also why regular marriage counseling is helpful. It's a dedicated time and space for communication. I know seeing a counselor for your marriage has a stigma attached to it, but think about it this way: If someone asked where you had been and you told them you were at a golf lesson, they'd think that's pretty cool and that you're really dedicated to getting better at it. Marriage counseling is no different. Making space for marriage counseling just shows you're committed to getting better at marriage.

I think that's why prayer is so powerful too. Prayer is just communicating with God. When we take unhurried time and space to speak openly and honestly with Him, it can reveal what's really happening in our hearts. Maybe that's why God can feel so silent sometimes when we're praying; He's a really good listener.

Get intentional about leaving space to communicate with those who are most important in your life. Don't try to hurry the conversation along. Show love by offering margin for communication.

Strategic Space

For several years, I led four-month backpacking trips through Asia and Central America. Most of the time, my teams thought I had the whole trip planned out. But I didn't. I nailed down the round-trip flights and the first week or two of the adventure. But that was it. Some of the more Type-A team members were always asking me to give them the "plan." I told them I do that on a need-to-know basis, but the truth was, I didn't actually know the entire plan. I'm a Type-A person, but I learned early on that it's important to leave open space in our schedule. Mainly because traveling, especially in the developing world, requires tons of flexibility. But also, some of the most memorable experiences—sleeping in yurts on the Mongolian steppe, exploring recently discovered ancient ruins in the jungles of Central America—never would have happened if I hadn't left space. They came up in the last minute, but we had space to seize the opportunities.

Not filling every moment also meant there were days when we didn't have anything to do. But I don't regret those days. In fact, some of the best talks I had with team members—life-changing, course-altering talks—came on those days. On one stretch of down days, a girl on our team realized she wasn't supposed to marry the guy she was engaged to and broke it off! Doing "nothing" gave her time to really figure out what she wanted. Sometimes doing nothing is the most valuable thing you can do.

When was the last time you had nothing to do? Literally nothing?

I think it's really hard for some of us to slow down and take a day to do nothing because we feel like we're being irresponsible. There are always more "things" we could do. Some people worry that they'll get left behind if they do nothing. We tend to pride ourselves on how busy we are, as if that means we're accomplishing something valuable. I once heard Bob Goff say, "It's easy to confuse a lot of activity with a purposeful life." I tend to believe that staying busy justifies my existence. I can even convince myself that what I'm doing is for God—it's God's work. But honestly, a lot of what I fill my time with is just my own attempt to keep from feeling worthless, bored, or out of control of my life.

I know that some reading this will look around and think, *It's just not possible to create more space or align where I am with the values I really want*. Sports schedules, debt, obligations, and/or our work schedules just won't allow it. I get it. Sometimes other people's decisions, betrayal, bureaucracy, and just plain obnoxiousness can put you in positions where it feels like survival mode is your only option. I completely understand. There will be seasons of challenge, some circumstances in which you just can't create more space in your time, money, or energy. But don't give up hope.

Rather than become resentful or depressed, in that moment, ask yourself what small step you can take to get closer to the target. Aim low. What small thing could you stop doing to make some space? Maybe there's something you enjoy, but it's just sapping too much of your time, money, or energy or stealing your joy in this season. Could you let it go for a while? It won't be forever. But for now, maybe it's creating more stress than it's worth.

Once you've taken that small step, look up and reevaluate. What's the next small step you can take? Sooner or later, if you keep taking small steps toward the target, you'll get close enough to hit it—and you'll be able to create some breathing room. Once you've got some breathing room and space, guard it. Create some boundaries to protect your new-found freedom.

6

Boundaries

"No" is a complete sentence.

—Anne Lamott

He would always call at the worst possible time, right before dinner. He was driving home from work—always time he had free, but it was really inconvenient for us.

For some reason, I regularly answered his calls. He'd pour out his struggles and ask my advice. He always seemed to have a crisis. I enjoyed helping him troubleshoot, but his calls always came during prime time with my family.

I started to realize he had a pattern. We'd talk through a challenge, come up with some really practical and wise action steps for him to take . . . and then he'd call me back a few weeks later and tell me he had done the opposite of what we talked about. And he got bad results. So now he was calling to ask what he should do to fix what he had done.

He did this over and over—creating more and more debt for himself, severing multiple relationships, and just creating more unnecessary suffering in his life. His actions showed he didn't actually value my input. (Again, if you want to know what someone values, look at what they do— not what they say.) In fact, in many ways, he was abusing my most valuable asset—time.

When I finally realized this, I had an *aha!* moment.

I set up a boundary. I told him I would not be able to continue our long conversations at dinnertime because he didn't seem to value and respect my time. I loved him, but there were others in my life who deserved the time I was giving him. That boundary eased a point of tension in my life and helped me give more time to my family.

Now, don't get me wrong. We are called to carry each other's burdens.[1] At some point in life, we'll all need someone to carry extra weight for us. But the goal is to give them a break so they can get their strength back to carry the burden that's theirs to carry. That's what gives life meaning. Completely taking someone's burden away is actually unloving because it weakens them.

But if someone is determined to do things that create more weight in their backpack through bad decisions and then depends on others to constantly carry that weight, that shows a lack of respect for the people they're leaning on. It's the opposite of love. It's actually abuse.

And it's our responsibility to love those people enough to stop carrying weight that isn't ours to carry. If someone is taking valuable resources of time, money, or energy that should be going to those who are most important in our life, then things are out of balance. It's up to us to lovingly put up a boundary so our limited resources aren't being taken from those in the inner circle who deserve them most.

Boundaries are prioritized love.

Healthy boundaries ensure that those to whom we are called to give our best actually *get* the best. Even Jesus had an inner circle, and He always gave his best to those in that circle. Jesus set the example of boundaries. So let's look at the role prioritized love plays in keeping it light in our lives.

Jesus and Boundaries

Jesus was the most loving man who ever lived. He loved perfectly. But if you look at His actions and words, it's easy to start to think that, at times, He wasn't very loving. In fact, sometimes He seemed a bit exclusionary. Jesus hand-picked twelve disciples to whom He gave the greatest amount of His time. But even in that small group, He had a close inner circle of three—Peter, James, and John.

There were times when Jesus seemed to be enjoying immense success, with large crowds begging for His teaching and attention, but right in the middle of that hoopla, He would pull away with just His small group. He'd leave the masses and go teach His inner circle. He was very selective about how He used his time and energy.

What's really confusing is, some of His most profound teaching was only shared with that small group of insiders. There's an interesting little linguistic clue that you see throughout the gospels that can revolutionize the way you read Jesus's words. You'll often see lines like, "Then he left the crowds and went into the house. And his disciples came with him."[2] When you see a reference to Him entering a house or going inside, pay close attention, because He's about to reveal some powerful insider knowledge to His inner circle—which I think is another picture of what healthy boundaries look like.

There are certain things that need to be kept "in the house." We only have so much time, money, and energy. There are certain parts of us that should primarily be reserved for those who have been placed within our realm of primary responsibility. I think that's part of what Jesus meant by one of His harshest statements: "Don't throw pearls before swine."[3] He's saying: Be wise about who you give your best to.

Speaking of harsh, one of Jesus's most savage moments took place when He left His home turf and headed to a neighboring region. While He was there, a woman begged Him to heal her daughter. Jesus's response doesn't seem very Christ-like. He ignored her at first, then when she asked again, said,

> "I was sent only to the lost sheep of the house of
> Israel."
> But she came and knelt before him, saying,
> "Lord, help me."

And he answered, "It is not right to take the children's bread and throw it to the dogs."[4]

Did Jesus just compare that woman to a dog? Why on earth was He so cold-hearted?

I have no doubt that this story, like all Scripture, has multiple layers of truth to it. But Jesus's response starts to make some sense to me when I see it in terms of boundaries. His primary mission in that season was to bring the message of salvation "to the Jew first and also to the Gentile."[5] There was a process and perfect timing to God's work. Right then, the Jews were His primary focus. Later, Peter—who was part of Jesus's inner circle of three—would be sent to Cornelius to open the gates to Gentiles,[6] and Paul would be sent to them after that. But at that time, Jesus had a primary mission: reach Israel.

This woman was not a Jew from Israel. But her response to Jesus showed Him she truly understood His mission and values. She said, "Yes, Lord, yet even the dogs eat the crumbs that fall from their master's table." Then Jesus answered her, "O woman, great is your faith! Be it done for you as you desire." And her daughter was healed instantly.[7] (Interestingly,

Jesus did many miracles for non-Jews when they showed faith in Him. In fact, many of His moments of greatest amazement at human faith came in response to something a Gentile said.)

Jesus had strong boundaries, but He also knew when to lower one to extend love at the right time and in the right way. He is our model. Healthy boundaries prioritize giving our best to those in our direct realm of responsibility first, but willingly extend beyond those at appropriate times, in the right amount. Boundaries are a wise prioritization of where our best efforts should go in each moment.

Not everything we have should be for everyone all the time. Not everyone should be a close friend. Not everyone should get our time, money, and energy. We are limited. We can't give the world everything it needs. Humility acknowledges that we will never save the world. Fortunately, Someone already did—Jesus. Our job is to simply seek His Kingdom regarding where to prioritize our time, money, and energy in the name of love.

I know I'm gonna get some pushback on the idea that we should hold back something from others—especially generosity or care. And I'm not saying we should make stinginess a lifestyle. I'm saying it requires wisdom and guidance from the Holy Spirit. Two things can be true at once. We're called to show love, but love doesn't always mean giving everything to everyone all at once. True compassion requires wisdom. Love always does what's best for the other person. It means extending love to him or her in the form they need most, at the time they need it most. And that's tricky.

Love has many faces. Sometimes love means looking the other way. Sometimes love requires confronting someone who is harming themselves and others. Sometimes love means rescuing someone time and again. Sometimes love requires letting them experience the pain of their bad decisions and then being there to help them regain their footing when they're ready to move forward.

Figuring out what love looks like in each situation depends on lots of factors. It's a lot easier to just go to one extreme or another. We tend to either have really strict boundaries with no room for anyone or anything else ("You shall not pass!"), or we have no boundaries and say yes to everything. Some of us need permission to establish strong boundaries; others need to open themselves up a little to others and extend beyond themselves. That's why it requires prayer, seeking counsel, and guidance from the Holy Spirit. It's not easy, but it's absolutely necessary.

When we develop a habit and reputation for having wise, healthy boundaries, it actually creates healthier and stronger relationships. It gives the most important people in our lives a sense of safety that allows them to flourish.

When boundaries are clear, it removes fear.

When Boundaries Are Clear

I'll never forget the place I was standing when it happened: the hallway between the kitchen and living room in our house. I was yelling at my mom for something. My father appeared from around the corner and, in a stern voice (something he rarely used), said, "Hey! That's my wife you're talking to. She'll be with me way after you're gone. You show her the respect she deserves."

In that moment, I realized that my dad loved my mom way more than me. And honestly, it was kind of reassuring. Knowing that my parents were more committed to each other than to me brought a lot of security. His commitment to prioritize her over me helped me feel safe—which is something all kids need.

There's a classic study (with lots of iterations) involving a new school built near a busy road. When the school opened, there was no fence. When kids were let out for recess, they'd all stay really close to the building. Eventually, a fence was built, and the kids naturally ventured out all the way up to the road. The security of the fence gave them the freedom to roam and play within those boundaries and helped them feel safe. Boundaries create a sense of safety and predictability.

Kids aren't the only ones who need safety to grow—we all do. We need the certainty that some structures around us are solid and predictable. Boundaries give us the freedom to know where we can and can't go. That's why Solomon said: "Do not move an ancient boundary stone set up by your ancestors."[8] If we destroy a boundary that has been standing for centuries—like traditional marriage or guarding the innocence of children—we do so at our peril. As much as we may push against the boundaries, deep down, we know they offer us a sense of security. We were made to need and want boundaries.

When kids know their parents aren't going to abandon them or each other, it gives them confidence. When our children and spouse know they're more important than our job or boss's demands, they feel valued and loved. When family knows they get our best energy and focus—even if it seems like they take it for granted—you can be confident it is building a strong foundation of trust in them that will give them a solid set of values on which to build their own lives. Most importantly, when it's clear that God's values are first in your life, your family will see it and feel a sense of confidence and courage to stand on that foundation too.

When healthy boundaries aren't clear, or are misplaced, it breeds anxiety and chaos. It also causes serious damage. I've met many people who felt they weren't safe at home because their "loving" parents were constantly welcoming strangers, or youth groups, or anyone who needed help into their house. I've heard horror stories of kids who were abused by those guests the parents allowed in with no vetting or caution. In their misguided compassion for the world, they actually harmed those for whom they had primary responsibility. They sacrificed their own children for a boundaryless kind of love. It looked like love to the outsider, but it was not prioritized love, and it actually turned into the abuse of those closest to them.

I know it's hard to believe that any act of seemingly sincere love could turn into abuse, but we're complex creatures and very prone to self-delusion. If we aren't constantly evaluating *why* we're doing what we're doing, even what seems most loving can end up causing pain if our boundaries don't match up with what God values.

I've talked to exasperated wives who can't get their husbands to confront their meddling mothers. The mother-in-law refuses to let go of her place of primary importance in her son's life and uses manipulation and criticism to constantly cause drama and frustration. The husband refuses to create a boundary and "leave his father and his mother and hold fast to his wife"[9] to protect the unity in his marriage. Some men have mother-in-laws who do the same thing. It can be challenging to figure out how to honor parents who have unhealthy boundaries or intrude on your marriage, but we have to make the effort to lovingly confront the issue—even if it's uncomfortable.

If you're an in-law, remember that when two people get married, they create a new family. It's fun to think we're "getting a new son or daughter," but the reality is they're becoming a unique unit and will need boundaries to establish their own values. This is hard for mothers, as they instinctively want to constantly nurture their kids—which is imperative and necessary when they're young. But our responsibility level needs to shift when our kids become adults. We can't protect and nurture them forever. In many ways, a failed mother—one who has released the child they'd rather nurture forever—is a successful mother. At some point, children have to break free and take responsibility for themselves.

Possibly the most tragic thing I've witnessed are pastors who neglect their families because one or both parents are busy doing "the Lord's work." A. W. Tozer was an amazing teacher and preacher whose writings impacted the spiritual walk of millions. After he died, his widow married a businessman. Someone asked her what it was like to be married to a man in business rather than ministry. She said something pretty potent: "I have never been happier in my life. Aiden (A. W. Tozer) loved Jesus Christ, but Leonard Odam (her new husband) loves me."[10] *Ouch!* Our relationship with the Lord should be of utmost importance, but we show the health of that relationship by how we love those in our circle of responsibility.

Boundaries are simply prioritized love.

That's why, once you've identified your priorities in this season, it's imperative that you establish clear boundaries that will protect what you value most. Here are a few boundaries I think are extremely important to always protect.

1. Commitment through Marriage

I'm convinced marriage is the second most important relationship anyone can ever commit to—just under our relationship to God in the values hierarchy. "Marriage should be honored by all, and the marriage bed kept pure."[11] Anyone or anything that infringes upon a marriage relationship needs to be confronted aggressively and thoroughly. Whether that's other people, previous romantic relationships, social media, work, in-laws, golf, video games, or even your own kids—if they're impacting your relationship with your spouse in a way that creates division or divided loyalties, it needs to be addressed, posthaste.

Another important element of this marriage boundary extends to protecting our children. I've worked with countless women and men who, after a divorce, began dating again. They would bring anyone they were dating into their home to meet and interact with their kids. The relationship would end, and a week later the kids would be meeting a new potential mate for their parent. This process creates tremendous uncertainty and fear in children, causing them to act out or become reclusive. At worst, it can lead to abuse.

"But Joël, don't I have a right to find love again?" you may ask. Yes, I hear you and I want that for you, too. But in your quest to find love, don't lower the boundaries that protect your primary responsibility to your kids. They will always be your kids. Until marriage is in place as a boundary, we endanger the emotional health of our children by parading a constant stream of new romantic interests in front of them.

2. Personal Values and Standards

If you're allowing people into your life who undermine or push you to compromise God's standards and values—morally, ethically—you need to love those people from a distance.

"Do not be deceived: 'Bad company ruins good morals.'"[12] We have to be selective about those we allow into our inner circle. They will influence us. One bad apple really can spoil the batch. In his classes on success, Jim Rohn often said, "You are the average of the five people you spend the most time with." We tend to think we're among the smarter ones in our group of friends, but really we're probably average. If you really are the smartest person in the room, you need to find a new room because there's a good chance you aren't being pushed to be the highest version of yourself in a group of people who don't have similar boundaries and standards as you.

3. Respect for Time and Wisdom

If someone who is not in your inner circle is taking your time and energy or asking for your wisdom but showing no respect for what you're giving them, it needs to be addressed. Time and emotional energy are limited resources; giving them to others means you'll have less to give to those in your primary circle of responsibility. Again, sometimes people need a little extra care and time. But if the ongoing relational pattern is one of them constantly taking but not respecting what you're offering, the most loving thing you can do is to back away from that relationship. You don't have to be mean about it. Just express that the time you're giving them needs to go to those to whom you have greatest commitment right now.

If that person gets angry or rejects you, that's a good sign the relationship was probably not healthy to start with. The people who truly have your best in mind will respect and value your boundaries.

When to Extend the Boundary

When a friend of mine found out she had cancer, she called a group of us together and gave a very curt explanation of what she expected from us:

- No stories about other people and their cancer.
- No health antidotes that "worked for a friend."
- No comments about how to drum up faith to get healed, etc.
- No personal spiritual interpretations about why this was happening.

The list was so long that, when she was done laying it out, we were all terrified to even talk to her about it. So no one did.

Having personally received a negative health diagnosis, I understand why she was so intense about laying down ground rules: People say the most ridiculous (and stupid) things to people who are sick. I'm convinced most of what they say is actually a projection of their own fears onto the person dealing with the illness. But I digress.

Bottom line: Because my friend went overboard in establishing what she thought was a boundary, it actually created a wall that led to isolation for her. And isolation is precisely the opposite of what you need when carrying the burdens of life. The Apostle Paul tells us to "bear one another's burdens."[13] But we can't do that if there's a giant wall between us and others.

Harvard University researcher Shawn Achor concluded that "the people who survive stress the best are the ones who actually increase their social investments in the middle of stress, which is the opposite of what most of us do."[14] In study after study, he found that social connection trumped all other variables in predicting someone's ability to weather difficult times. Building a wall that you call a boundary in order to avoid the discomfort that can come in relationships can actually sabotage your ability to succeed in difficult situations.

If a boundary is creating isolation, it's unhealthy. And if you haven't been willing to invest in others from time to time by extending your boundaries, there's a good chance you'll feel completely alone when a crisis hits. Healthy boundaries are malleable and can be extended to welcome people and experiences in each season of life.

When Jesus lowered His boundary for the woman who asked for His help, He first evaluated her commitment level. Her persistence showed she valued Him and His time and energy. When someone shows they respect our values, it's okay to lower a boundary—even if only temporarily.

Know this: There will always be people who cannot offer reciprocity—emotionally, financially, or in other ways—because of their own lack. If those people are in your direct realm of responsibility, you'll need to figure out a healthy way to balance giving to them without holding them back from learning to take their own responsibility. A healthy boundary involves give and take: It creates a healthy ecosystem of giving and receiving from each other and feeds mutual growth.

The higher you rise, the tighter your inner circle needs to be. But those relationships have to be formed and nurtured through years of relationship. If you're looking for people for your inner circle once you've arrived at some level of "success," it will be hard to distinguish who is truly a friend and who just wants to be part of your success. Our two greatest priorities should always be our relationship with God and our relationships with people. Make sure you're investing in those you meet along the journey to success. Because, the truth is, healthy relationships are a sign of true success.

Draw the Line

Let me ask you a question: Is it possible that some of the major tension points in your life could be eliminated if you had the courage to establish some loving and wise boundaries, then stick to them? Could some of the stress you feel in your most important relationships be lessened if those people were confident that you really prioritized them over other things that demand your time, money, and energy?

Establishing and maintaining good boundaries is always a moving target. Some boundaries will change over time. People who were once in your inner circle may need to be loved from a distance for a while. Folks who were outside the circle may need to be brought in for a while. Kids will need to be released from our care (a bit) once they get married. Seek God's wisdom and wise counsel as you navigate which boundaries you need right now to make sure your love is prioritized correctly.

If you honestly can't figure out if a boundary is out of place (or nonexistent), just ask the people who are closest to you—your inner circle. They know.

The great news is, when your boundaries are heathy, it frees up time, money, and energy. You'll find freedom you may never have known was possible.

That kind of freedom always starts on the inside. And that's why, if you really want lasting change in your life, it's important to take some time for self-discovery.

7

Self-Discovery

A humble knowledge of thyself is a surer way to
God than a deep search after learning.

—Thomas à Kempis

I spoke at a pastors' conference recently. A giant man came up to me afterward and said, "Nice talk, but I don't really buy into all that psychology stuff you talked about. I take things as they are and trust that the Bible is enough."

I was tempted to react, but I just said, "Hmm. Amen, brother."

He began rambling about the sufficiency of Scripture (things I totally agreed with, for the most part). I just listened.

As the conversation continued, he said casually, "Yeah, my wife told me if I don't come back from this conference willing to make some changes, she's gonna divorce me." He looked off into the distance.

"Oh wow!" I acted surprised. "What's her complaint?"

He shared a series of complaints, all relating to his unwillingness to be more sensitive to people's needs, and his hard-headedness and inflexibility.

We talked about his situation for a few minutes, but he didn't seem to have any desire to look a little deeper for the root cause of the problem. He really thought the problem was his wife, not him. After all, he was faithfully serving the Lord and his congregation and thought his wife just "needed to submit to the Word of God."

I listened as long as I could. "Well, let me pray for you," I finally said. "Sounds like you've got some soul searching to do." (I didn't bother to point out that in the Bible, the Greek word for "soul" is *psuche*, which is where we get the word "psychology.")

I wanted to feel sorry for that guy, but it was hard. It seemed like his unwillingness to look a little deeper into himself was causing major issues in his family (and probably his church), but he wasn't even able, or willing, to connect those dots.

I'm sure you've met a handful of people who regularly leaving you thinking: *What is their deal? How do they not see what they're doing?*

We all have friends, family, and coworkers who seem oblivious to how their actions or viewpoints are hurting themselves or those around them. We all know someone who can't ever admit they messed up or got something wrong. They can't see that always having to have the last word and be "right" is driving people away from them. We have friends who would be pleasant to be around if they'd just stop trying to convince us they're worth hanging around with. Sometimes they're sabotaging their own success. It's clear as day to us, but they're just so insecure or fearful that they can't even see it. But everyone else does.

The funny thing is, there's a good chance others are asking the same things about us. If there's enough tension building in those relationships, we may even be asking that about ourselves: *What is my deal? Why do I always do that?*

We all have quirks, fears, and insecurities that create unnecessary suffering in our relationships. When it comes to keeping it light in our lives, a lack of self-awareness—not taking the time to figure out what is driving our behavior—can create lots of burdens and block our path forward. But it doesn't have to.

A little self-awareness about what's going on inside us can actually free us from the weight of self-sabotage and insecurity. Because how we respond to the world around us is always a result of something happening deep within us.

King Solomon said, "The purpose in a man's heart is like deep water, but a man of understanding will draw it out."[1] We all have a deep well of experiences, personality traits, fears, hopes, and dreams that lie just below the surface. Solomon is saying that taking things "as they are" isn't enough if you want to be wise.

There's a deeper level to every person that drives what we do. We tend to have a consistent pattern in the way we interact with the world. How you approach anything tends to be how you approach everything.

Your thoughts, emotions, and desires (your soul) impact how you respond to the world. If you're just taking things "as they are," it's easy to spend your whole life in survival mode—reacting to what's happening and running away from pain, rather than wisely evaluating what can be done to change the situation on a deeper level. When we don't deal with our deeper issues, we're really prone to find ourselves feeling overwhelmed time and again, asking, "Why does this keep happening to me?"

At some point, if we really want lasting change, we need to dig up the root cause of why we keep getting into situations where we feel overwhelmed and stressed out. When we can identify what's motivating us to take on more than we need to, we can learn to keep things in balance. That's why a little self-discovery is imperative if you really want to keep it light.

What Are You Seeking?

I've taken lots of people on adventure trips in dozens of countries, often in some pretty challenging environments. My team members come from all walks of life, all socioeconomic levels, and very diverse backgrounds. Seeing people in challenging and tense situations has taught me a lot about human nature. (And some of it's not pretty!)

One of the most important things I learned early on is that no matter who the person is or where they're from, people can endure pretty much any challenge if they're fed well and know where they're going to sleep. No matter what challenges we face while hiking, rafting, or sailing, if those basic needs are covered, the team members can handle pretty much any challenge. When they don't get those things, the trip gets tense in a hurry.

Human beings are infinitely complex. But at the same time, when you get right down to it, we're all seeking the same things. In fact, I've found that what we're seeking can be narrowed down to three specific things. We're all seeking:

1. Security: physical, financial, emotional, and relational safety
2. Connection: relationship with others, being seen, esteemed, heard, valued, and accepted
3. Empowerment: having some control, choices, and autonomy

Every hope and dream we have for ourselves and our families comes down to one of those three roots. A better job, the new house, the dream marriage, the promotion, college for your kids, and padding that 401(k) retirement account are all aimed, in one way or another, at achieving security, connection, and empowerment.

There's nothing wrong with you for wanting those things. Wanting them doesn't mean you're weak or incapable—it just means you're human. We were created to need those things. Before Adam and Eve ate the forbidden fruit, they lived in a state of perfect fulfillment. God met all their needs in a perfect way.

They had security. They lived in a perfect environment with nothing to harm them.

They had perfect connection with each other and even with God Himself—so much so that God walked with them in the cool of the day.

They were totally empowered and had control of the whole garden. They had the run of the place.

God just asked them to not do one thing: Don't eat from one tree. But they fell for a lie and misused their control. As soon as they did, the perfect security, connection, and empowerment they had from God were replaced with fear and shame. They felt naked and vulnerable—and we've all been feeling that ever since.

The story of Adam and Eve explains why we all live with the fear of not getting those three needs met. We all feel insecure and inadequate, concerned we won't have what we need. We feel incomplete. And that leads to insecurity.

Never forget this: Every human being feels insecure. That pushy, loud boss of yours—insecure. He just tries to hide it with aggression and attempting to convince everyone he's right all the time. That happy, never-discouraged friend—insecure. She just hides it with people-pleasing and humor.

Even the strongest of us feel like we aren't enough at times. At some point, we all feel like outsiders. In psychology, we call this "imposter syndrome." You can try to build your self-esteem all you want, but deep down there's a voice that says you aren't what you should be.

That feeling of not being enough is *shame*. Guilt says, "I did something wrong." Shame is deeper; it says, "There is something wrong with *me*." Deep down, we know the world is not what it should be, and neither are we. And just like Adam and Eve, we feel vulnerable and afraid that our needs won't be met. That's a big reason why we all tend to keep adding things to our backpack in life.

But fear is a horrible motivation. It drives us to carry more than we should and threatens our ability to trust God. We're prone to give our best resources to anything that offers us freedom from that fear—money, power, relationships, or substances that numb the discomfort. We're all susceptible to becoming slaves to our fear. That's why Paul was so adamant when he said, "It is for freedom that Christ has set us free. Stand firm, then, and do not let yourselves be burdened again by a yoke of slavery."[2]

Only God's love can offer perfect security, connection, and empowerment.

I've never really been content with pat answers to deep questions like, "God's love is all we need." It sounds like a pathetic greeting card. It's absolutely true, but how does that help when we've got bills that need to be paid, relationships in conflict, and jobs that are demanding more than we've got to give? We don't just have time to sit around and bask in how loved we are when life is weighing us down.

Enter Jesus. Again.

> "Therefore do not be anxious, saying, 'What shall we eat?' or 'What shall we drink?' or 'What shall we wear?' For the Gentiles seek after all these things, and your heavenly Father knows that you need them all. But seek first the kingdom of God and his righteousness, and all these things will be added to you."[3]

Jesus says He knows we're seeking security, connection, and empowerment. He even acknowledges that God knows we need them. But He says the path to getting those things we're seeking is to seek something higher: the Kingdom of God.

And this is the daily battle.

Every day, when life gets intense, we have to decide what we're going to seek first. Will we seek security, connection, and empowerment through brute force and our own power, or are we going to seek what God values and trust that He'll provide?

If I'm honest, I naturally tend to resort to my own power and control much of the time—which reveals a lot about me. Remember, how you do anything is how you tend to do everything. How we respond when life gets hard can be a great tool for helping us gain insight on where we're seeking our own way, rather than God's way, of dealing with the weight of life. When we know what we're seeking, it reveals where we are prone to not seek God's Kingdom, become fearful, and add more and more to our packs.

So let's look at how to identify what you're seeking.

Know Thyself

A few years ago, a pastor invited me to join the staff of his church. I instantly refused. He asked why I was so resistant. My answer was easy: "I don't want to be controlled." So he promised not to control me. But even though he was a friend, I didn't believe him. In my mind, *everyone* wants to control me! I'm not kidding. I really do believe everyone wants to control me—and that fear of being controlled, along with how my personality is wired, tends to drive every decision I make.

Thankfully, I actually sought God's desires on the offer, rather than mine, and ended up accepting the job. I went into it ready to jump ship at the first sign of being controlled. But amazingly, that never happened. More importantly, that offer changed my life! I can honestly say I never could've imagined the fulfillment working for that pastor has brought. But I never would have experienced it if I had not sought God, rather than my own desire to be in total control. I only knew what I was running from: being controlled. God knew what I needed more than I did. In seeking Him, I got what I really wanted and needed.

That is the danger of being driven by fear: We tend to miss out on really great things God has for us. But when we seek Him above our need for security, connection, and control, it opens us up to amazing possibilities.

I'm always seeking empowerment and control. What are you seeking? Security, connection, empowerment?

What you're seeking influences how you respond to the world, which opportunities you pursue, and what you run from. What you're seeking stems from lots of variables: your personality, temperament, and past experiences. Typically, we seek one specific thing more than others. When anything threatens my empowerment or control in a situation, I go into beast mode. I do whatever it takes to make sure I'm not controlled.

A big part of self-awareness is recognizing how our personality and past experiences (nature and nurture) come together to form how we approach the world. When we understand the role this combination plays, it helps us see where we may have a distorted view of reality. It can also help us see where fear is causing us to run from, rather than toward, something. Fear is always a heavy burden that slows us down and hinders us from what God has for us. Seeking greater self-awareness is essentially what King David did when he said, "Search me, God, and know my heart; test me and know my anxious thoughts."[4]

Paying attention to what makes us fearful or anxious—as much as we may want to ignore it—can help us look a little deeper (into that deep well) to see what's going on inside us. Typically, what you fear most points to where you may be seeking your own security, connection, and empowerment over seeking God's Kingdom. In the words of Carl Jung, "Where your fear is, there is your task."[5]

If you're seeking security, either because of personality or past experiences, you're prone to settle for guarantees rather than living by faith. Anything of great value in life is going to come with some risk. It will require stepping out in faith, unsure of the outcome, and trusting God. But if you have to have everything perfectly secure before you move forward, you'll probably never move forward. I've seen way too many people stay at jobs that are unfulfilling and draining because those jobs offer security. Others stay in abusive relationships for the same reason.

Sometimes we get so focused on our security that we end up ignoring the needs of those around us. This can lead to self-absorption and narcissism. The driving force behind narcissism tends to be an early experience of abandonment, creating an overwhelming need for security. Seeking security is natural, but if it motivates us more than seeking God's Kingdom and walking by faith, it will become a burden that holds us back.

Seeking connection and esteem from others can quickly turn into people-pleasing and a lack of boundaries. Eventually, if left unchecked, that burden will turn to resentment. Approval addiction is an unbearable weight to carry. Being obsessed with connection can also lead to unhealthy dependence on alcohol, drugs, or shopping—a connection point that's always there for you to help take the edge off when life gets hard.

When you're seeking connection, you tend to be driven by a fear of rejection. But God's love will never reject you. And, as ethereal as it sounds, when you find your primary connection in God's love for you, it actually empowers you to connect better with others. When your sense of acceptance and connection comes from God, you'll be able to love others without strings attached or needing their affirmation. You'll love others out of an overflow of His love for you, and giving to them won't wear you out.

If you're like me in seeking empowerment or control, understand that it can lead to perfectionism and a fear of being embarrassed or humiliated. You'll be shouldering the heavy burden of trying to look like you have it together all the time. You'll try to control everything. Which, in an imperfect world, is a recipe for perpetual frustration. There are some things in life you'll never control—God being one of them. Honestly, that's my constant battle with God: He won't let me control Him! I have to surrender all the time to the fact that God is going to do what He's going to do, but I can trust His motives no matter what.

As simple and trite as it sounds, here's a truth you can hang your hat on: If you're seeking security, connection, and empowerment over God's Kingdom, you'll always be carrying a heavy burden. But if you're seeking His Kingdom and what He values above everything else, you'll get everything you're seeking—and more—but the burden will be light.

Know thyself. Not so you can become self-obsessed. Know yourself so you can recognize what's getting in the way of seeking God's Kingdom.

It will take some work. We're all prone to self-deception and to thinking we're something we aren't. Recognizing what you do and don't have is a form of stewardship; self-awareness is stewardship of how God made us. It's knowing what we have to work with and what has the potential to limit us.

The Apostle Paul talked about this when he said, "But by the grace of God I am what I am, and his grace toward me was not in vain."[6] He points out that God took his misguided motivations and turned them for righteous purposes. The same is true for you: God made you who you are and gave you the experiences you've had for a reason. His grace is what redeems our motivations and experiences and turns them for His purposes.

When we become more self-aware while seeking God's Kingdom, we actually become a greater blessing to those around us.

Self-Awareness vs. Self-Focus

I spent a lot of time in the principal's office when I was in high school. Typically, it was because I had spoken out about something I thought was just plain wrong. I'd boldly comment on it in what was seen as a disrespectful manner (and might actually have been) to the teacher or administrator, and end up being sent to the office.

This happened a lot.

I'll never forget something my dad said as we walked out of one of those meetings. "Joël, one of these days that outspokenness is gonna be a gift. But right now, it just gets you into a lot of trouble." My dad always affirmed my willingness to speak up about things no one else wanted to talk about. But not many others did at the time. So I grew up feeling like there was a part of my personality that wasn't good. I felt a constant pressure to rein it in and not speak up. But when I didn't speak up, I felt really compromised, like I was lying. To quietly sit by and submit to something wrong felt . . . wrong!

It wasn't until I was in my thirties that I realized the thing I thought was a curse—the need to speak out—was actually a gift. Now, obviously God had to refine that drive within me. I had to learn that sometimes you need to be quiet because you don't know all the facts. But it was quite a liberating moment when I started to see how my personality really was something I could use to help other people. In fact, much of what I do today flows from that gift: speaking up about things most people would rather ignore.

That drive has been in me since I was a kid, and I'm

convinced God put it there. But it needed to be sanctified—turned around for God's purposes. When I use it improperly—for my own empowerment and control rather than for others—it causes me all sorts of burdens. When I use it correctly—seeking God's Kingdom and His righteousness—it can still feel like a burden, but it's a burden that can actually bless others. And that's the difference between self-awareness and self-focus. Self-focus is used for ourselves; self-awareness helps us bless others.

Jesus was pretty emphatic when He said: "If anyone would come after me, let him deny himself and take up his cross and follow me."[7] This line is often used to tell people to forget or ignore themselves so they can be Jesus-focused. I get what they're saying, and I agree, mostly. Self-awareness can easily turn to self-focus. Self-awareness can be kind of addictive. There's something liberating about discovering our deeper motivations. It opens our eyes and helps us understand ourselves better. You've probably met people who are on a constant quest to "find themselves" by reading loads of self-help books and doing the most *en vogue* personality profile. They're constantly focused on learning more about themselves so they can bask in their uniqueness. But this can quickly turn to self-focus. That's what Jesus calls us to deny, the kind of awareness that leads only to looking inward.

But I also believe denying something God placed in us is shortsighted. Yes, we all have quirks and sinful patterns. We're all prone to seeking something from the wrong motives. Sin is always a perversion of something good that God created. Our search for security, connection, and empowerment is ultimately us seeking God's perfect love. The goal isn't to get rid of our natural drives and motives; it's to become aware of them and allow God to sanctify them—to turn them into something He can use for His Kingdom and righteousness.

But you'll never be able to get serious about turning those drives over to God's Kingdom if you refuse to recognize them. In fact, you'll probably find yourself bumping into the same problems in your relationships and thought processes over and over again, feeling guilty, and wondering why you just can't seem to get ahead. But self-awareness brings freedom.

Self-awareness is recognizing that it is:

by grace you have been saved through faith. And this is not your own doing; it is the gift of God, not a result of works, so that no one may boast. For

> we are his workmanship, created in Christ Jesus
> for good works, which God prepared beforehand,
> that we should walk in them.[8]

God made us and saved us. That's nothing we can brag about—it's all Him. In response to His saving work in our lives, we want to turn what we're seeking over to Him and trust that He will use our natural drives for his purposes. Self-awareness is about recognizing our core motivations, fears, and perspectives and aligning them with God's Kingdom. When we do, He uses them for His purposes.

Let God transform your motivations and past experiences for His purposes, and you'll find life gets a lot more meaningful. You'll go from protecting and defending yourself and what you've got to serving others and giving freely.

That's why it's so important to figure out exactly what is motivating you. So let me ask you a question: If you had to narrow it down to one word, what would you say you're seeking most?

Security? Connection? Empowerment?

How do you approach things in your life? Do you seek guarantees and sure bets? Then maybe you're seeking security or empowerment. Do you seek acceptance and approval from others? Maybe you're seeking connection. Are you driven to appear successful, in control, and put together? Maybe you're seeking empowerment.

Here's a big question: What do most of your fears and anxiety tend to be about? Your fear points to your task.

Figure out what you're seeking, and you'll find what's prone to adding more weight to your shoulders than God intends for you to carry. You'll also figure out what's holding you back from the freedom God wants you to have.

Still not sure what you're seeking?

Ask someone who knows you well—they'll have an outside perspective. Ask them: *What do you think is holding me back from all God wants for me?*

Refuse to get offended by their answer. And don't write off what they say, even if they don't say it in the most perfect or kind way. Consider it. We learn who we are and who we can be in relationship with other people. In fact, I don't think we can figure out who God made us to be on our own. We learn who we are and what drives us by being in community with others. Ask for their input.

Above all else, make the words of the psalmist a regular prayer:

> Search me, God, and know my heart;
> test me and know my anxious thoughts.
> See if there is any offensive way in me,
> and lead me in the way everlasting.
> (Psalm 139:23–24)

In fact, I'd encourage you to read all of Psalm 139—it's all about self-awareness and our relationship with God.

Know thyself.

8

Consistency

*Success is neither magical nor mysterious. Success
is the natural consequence of consistently apply-
ing basic fundamentals.*

—*Jim Rohn*

To start this chapter, I was trying to come up with a story of a time when I waited for something way longer than I had expected to be forced to wait before I received it. So I asked my wife if she could think of an example. Her response was telling: "You think everything takes longer than it should!"

Alas, she is right.

I'm guessing you can relate. We all have an area in our lives where we're asking: *Why is this taking so long?*

Why is it taking so long to dig myself out of this financial debt?

Why is it taking so long for my son or daughter to come to their senses?

Why is it taking so long for me to find a spouse?

Why is it taking so long to get this relationship on track?

Even when we're seeking the Kingdom of God, life is hard. We're doing our best to make wise choices and honor Him, but oftentimes, we just aren't seeing the results we expected.

We live in a world where we can get pretty much anything we want in an instant. But there are some things in life that just don't come quickly. As hard as we push and try to make things happen, some things just don't happen on our timeline. And that can lead to lots of frustration and disappointment. "Hope deferred makes the heart sick."[1]

The weight of the wait can feel almost unbearable.

And, honestly, God seems to work way more slowly than I want Him to most of the time. I've heard it said that there are no microwaves in God's kitchen, only crockpots. God's work is rarely as quick as we want it to be—but it's always thorough and complete. In fact, His timing is perfect. But it doesn't come at the speed of light; it comes at the speed of a seed.

But you can be certain of this: If you consistently plant the right seeds, you will eventually see a harvest.

The Speed of a Seed

I started implementing the stuff I've shared in this book about values and sacrifice and focus into my own life about eight years ago. I am just now beginning to see some of the fruits of those decisions. I believe there's more to come, but it has been a slowly unfolding process—which fits pretty accurately with something Jesus said about seeking His Kingdom:

> "The kingdom of God is as if a man should scatter seed on the ground. He sleeps and rises night and day, and the seed sprouts and grows; he knows not how. The earth produces by itself, first the blade, then the ear, then the full grain in the ear. But when the grain is ripe, at once he puts in the sickle, because the harvest has come."[2]

That's how seeking the Kingdom of God works. It's a slow process that takes time.

Honestly, I don't like that. I don't know about you, but most of the time what I'm really hoping for is a magic trick. I want something to pop up from nothing. I want the strong relationship to magically appear. I want to win the lottery and have all the money I need without working for it. So I pray that God will use all of His power to give me what I want—right now. We hear just enough stories of this happening for people that we believe it will happen for us, too. But the truth is, the stories we hear of overnight success are never the full story. There are no overnight successes.

God works through processes. He uses The Law of the Farm that Jesus talked about in that verse you just read. Yes, God can do whatever He wants. He can easily make something from nothing. But more often than not, He uses the processes of sowing and reaping that He designed. This is actually a cause for great, rational hope. We can work hard, pray hard, and sleep hard knowing that God is working His processes behind the scenes at all times—even when we can't see it.

You can be certain that if you plant a seed, tend to it (steward it), and wait long enough, you are going to see a harvest.

When a seed grows, a large part of the important work of preparation happens below the surface, in the dark. In fact, how high and wide a plant grows depends greatly on how strong the root system is underneath it. But that root system grows in darkness and obscurity. The strength of what we see in the plant depends on the strength of what we don't see below the surface.

The same is true in life. It's the stuff nobody sees that brings the results everyone wants. If you see something that is healthy and strong, you can be certain that under the surface there's something just as healthy and strong—but you probably didn't see that. If you see ongoing success in someone's life, you can be certain there's a long backstory of hard work and discipline.

And that is the hard part. Because "No discipline seems pleasant at the time, but painful. Later on, however, it produces a harvest of righteousness and peace for those who have been trained by it."[3] Discipline is the ability to forgo instant gratification for a bigger payoff at the end: the fruit of righteousness. And, *voila*, there's that reminder of what we're called to seek again—God's Kingdom and His righteousness. It's about keeping our eyes on the Kingdom of God as our ultimate goal and trusting that pursing His values will pay off in the form of what we really want. When you stay disciplined and focused on that goal, you can be confident you'll receive a harvest.

Discipline is about keeping the end in mind. It's not how we start that matters, it's how we end. "The end of a matter is better than its beginning, and patience is better than pride."[4] Anyone can start strong, but finishing strong is a whole other ballgame. It requires what Eugene Peterson called "A Long Obedience in the Same Direction."

We can sacrifice, prioritize, set up boundaries, and gain self-awareness, but if we can't stay disciplined and consistent, it's all for naught. The ability to consistently focus on priorities over the long haul is what sets apart those who get overwhelmed and give up from those who go far in life.

The Power of Consistency

A guy named James Prochaska spent years studying how people change. He concluded that change happens in the following stages:

    1. Pre-contemplation: We're living our life, unaware

that change is needed. We may feel some tension, but we don't really think anything needs to happen—but others tend to see it.

2. Contemplation: We begin to realize there might be a problem, and we start thinking about what a healthy change might look like and what it would require.

3. Preparation: We start to take small steps toward making a change, dipping our toe into the new behavior.

4. Action: We move forward with new habits and patterns.

5. Maintenance: We stay consistent and focused on the new habits and pattern. When we stay consistent, we avoid relapsing into our old patterns.

As he developed this model, Prochaska found that right after the Action stage of making a change, a person could go one of two ways: Relapse or Maintenance. If you don't develop a solid pattern of consistency with the new value system, it's very easy to fall back into old patterns.

I've walked through this pattern quite a few times in my life. Unfortunately, on more than a few occasions, I fell back into my old habits of taking on too much and getting overwhelmed. That's why I tend to believe that most of the important work in life comes down to maintenance—consistently staying on track with what you've changed.

Anyone can make a change for a short time. It's the folks who stay consistent and maintain that change who go far in life.

When I was a teenager, a new shopping center opened in my city. A few years later, I took some friends back to that city with me and was raving about that shopping center. But when we got there, it was falling apart! The owners had spent lots of time, money, and energy building that place. It was amazing when it started, but nobody maintained it, and things fell apart. Our lives are no different. If we don't constantly focus on maintaining what we've worked to build in our lives, things will fall apart.

Maintenance is just as, if not more, important than building.

Never forget this: Success is a direction, not a destination. When you're seeking first the Kingdom of God, you're on the road of success. You can be certain that you'll reap a harvest. But it's not a one-time thing or destination. When you consistently value what God values, in the order He values it, you can be confident that eventually you will see something beautiful appear. That's why Paul reminds us: "And let us not grow weary of doing good, for in due season we will reap, if we do not give up."[5]

But that's the key: You have to keep doing what's right while you're waiting for the harvest, even if you get tired. You have to develop a routine that allows you to maintain a consistent level of intensity.

There are two things I've found that can quickly hijack our consistency: 1) not knowing your *why*, and 2) comparison.

When Your *Why* Is Clear

A few years ago, when I was first starting our ministry, a coach recommended I start a podcast. I agreed that I needed a podcast, but I didn't want to create even more work for myself. I also didn't want to spend hours looking for guests every week, and I didn't want to host it alone. Based on other projects I've done, I knew that taking on a weekly program could turn into a burden that actually got in the way of me giving my best in other areas. So for about five years, I didn't do a podcast.

But one day, I was talking to my dad about some things I had learned from him growing up. I realized that one day, he wouldn't be around anymore, and I really wanted my daughter to be able to hear his wisdom. That's when it hit me: *I needed to start a podcast where I talk to my dad about stuff I learned from him*. I knew that goal would give me the motivation I needed to stay consistent. We started doing that podcast four years ago, and it's no burden at all. In fact, I look forward to it every week! I love it when we get new listeners, and I'm grateful that people even listen, but honestly, I don't do it for that reason: I do it because I want to build a library of my dad's wisdom to pass on to my daughter.

Consistency becomes a lot easier when your *why* is clear. When you've filtered what you're doing right now through your values hierarchy—valuing what God values—it's much easier to stay disciplined when life gets hard. Some really confusing and challenging seasons will come and go, but when you've got a clear picture of why you're doing what you're doing, it's going to be a lot easier to stay consistent throughout those periods. In the words of Friedrich Nietzsche (a guy Christians don't quote much), "He who has a why to live can bear almost any how."[6]

If you're ever in doubt about your ultimate why—the one that should drive all your values—here it is: Our endgame as Christ-followers should be to hear the words: "Well done, good and faithful servant. You have been faithful over a little; I will set you over much. Enter into the joy of your master."[7] One day we'll stand before God and be rewarded for staying consistent and faithful in seeking His Kingdom.

The Comparison Trap

A few years ago, I took a team hiking on Hawaii's Na Pali Coast. I was out front most of the hike, but at one point I stepped aside to take a picture. I was kind of hidden and the team walked past me.

I fell in line behind them and was following closely. I normally hike at a fairly slow, steady pace but they were hiking really quickly, and I felt like I was running to keep up. We kept going faster and faster up the hills. I was exhausted and nearly just stopped going, but I kept thinking *I have to keep up or I'll look bad.*

We finally stopped at the top of an intense uphill section. I was panting hard. The guy leading turned around and gave me a look of shock. "What are you doing back there?" he said. "I've been trying to catch up with you and couldn't figure out how you were hiking so fast."

I think that's a good picture of what happens when we start to compare ourselves to others. It just leads to exhaustion and burnout. I wear myself out chasing after a particular person or thing that I think is setting the pace. I feel like I have to keep up or else I'll look bad. Meanwhile, it's quite possible that person thinks he's trying to keep up with me.

We each have our own trail to hike in life and our own speed at which to do it. We also have our own unique burden to bear on the way. Comparing our journey to others' will only lead to frustration and exhaustion. That's what the Apostle Paul was talking about when he said, "when they measure themselves by one another and compare themselves with one another, they are without understanding."[8]

Comparing yourself to others can be particularly frustrating when you feel like you're making tons of sacrifices and seeing no results. You try to be wise, discipline yourself, save money, and watch what you eat, but everyone else seems to be out living their best life and getting away with doing whatever they want. It can make you want to throw up your hands and just give up. The thing is, you don't see the price those people are paying behind the scenes, or will pay down the road.

I love social media. It allows us to share high moments in our lives with others. But much of what we see is a deceptive picture of what's actually happening. We don't see the entire story. It's all filtered. We start comparing ourselves to something that has a backstory we don't even know about.

A friend told me that he recently had to fire a guy for some shady stuff he was doing. He said the night he fired him, that guy got into the company's computers and stole lots of material before they could remove him from their accounts.

A few days later, I got a friend request on social media from the guy who had stolen the intellectual property. I looked at his posts; there was nothing about him getting fired, but there were loads of posts about how God was blessing his new coaching business and making it explode with growth. Hmm.

Around that same time, I heard from another friend, telling me about all the struggles in her life. She had lost her job. Her boyfriend, whom she had been dating while waiting for her divorce to finalize, had broken up with her. She was getting kicked out of her apartment and moving into a seedy motel. Later that day, the same girl posted a picture of herself sitting by a pool. It was the pool at the seedy motel—the only place she could afford—but you could only see the bright blue water and her legs kicked up on a lounger. She posted about how important self-care is and how she was living her best life. All sorts of people commented, "I wish I had your life." Hmm.

Having spent lots of hours listening to people in counseling, I've found that most of what they say so confidently is actually them trying to convince themselves that things are better than they actually are. We think by talking (or posting on social media). Most folks are trying to make sense of things in their heads by talking it out in public. Call me cynical, but now when I see someone posting a lot of pics or going overboard talking about how great their spouse is or how fulfilled they are, I just assume they're struggling.

I'm all for staying positive and looking at the bright side.

The problem is, while someone is trying to convince themselves and the world of how great their life is, we're all looking at the snapshot and comparing our own lives to it with no context for the bigger picture. What you see and hear—especially in these days of artificial intelligence and photoshop—can be extremely deceptive. Sometimes intentionally so, sometimes unintentionally. But either way, if we start comparing our journey to what we see in the lives of others, we will quickly lose focus on our unique path.

I have to remind myself that I'll never be all I could be if I spend my time comparing my life to others'. I don't know the whole burden they have to carry, and it's easy for me to start playing the victim when I think I have a heavier weight to carry than they do. My burden is *my* burden, and God has given me what I need to carry it. I just have to remain focused on my journey.

You'll never find peace if you're constantly comparing yourself to others. The only person you should compare yourself to is the person you were yesterday. Seek God's Kingdom with your life. Stay consistent, and you can be confident God will lead you right to your unique destiny.

Seek and You Will Find

In 1912, Hiram Bingham set out to find the lost Inca city of
Vilcabamba—a.k.a., El Dorado, the lost city of gold. Finding
El Dorado has long been the goal of many adventurers and
glory-seekers. Someone told Bingham about a hillside fortress
the Spanish conquistadors had never found, so he went to
explore the overgrown ruins. Bingham didn't find El
Dorado—but he did stumble upon Machu Picchu, and it
became his legacy. (Though he wasn't the first to actually find
it, he was the first to extensively document and excavate it.)
He never found the lost city of Vilcabamba, but he definitely
found a treasure worth his effort.

I think that's a good picture of what happens when we
stay consistently focused on seeking the highest good. When
you seek first the Kingdom of God and His righteousness in
every stage of the journey of life, you will find exactly what
you need to find. It may not be what you were expecting, but
the prize you find will be the one you needed. You can be certain of that. The key is to constantly seek the Kingdom—what
God values—in your life. But you must constantly *keep*
seeking.

When I got my master's degree in counseling, I was told

there were three or four different careers paths for which I could use it. The problem was, I didn't like any of those things! But I set out to honor God to the best of my ability and ended up doing whatever it is I do today. (Sometimes it's hard to explain exactly what that is.) I never would have imagined I could make a living doing what I do—writing, speaking, leading expeditions, and running a retreat center—but all those things materialized as I did my best to value what God values. He led me right to the fulfillment I was looking for.

The same will be true for you.

This is why consistent focusing on the right priorities is so important. It can take a while to find your "calling." It can take quite a few years to figure out what you're really gifted to do and what you probably should leave to someone else. But as you continue seeking what God values most in each season of life, learning how He's wired you, and just doing the best you can with what you have in front of you, you can be certain He will lead you to exactly what you're looking for.

Just remember it will come at the speed of a seed.

When I first started on the road to what I'm doing today, I had some big hopes and dreams. I was certain things were going to take off and I'd see massive success. But what I got for the first ten years was lots of disappointment and hard work that didn't seem to yield any results.

I got tired of having my dreams dashed to pieces—so much so that if something promising showed up on the horizon, I tried to not get my hopes up anymore. But I knew giving up wasn't an option. I've learned through hiking that you can get to the top of pretty much any mountain if you just keep putting one foot in front of another, so I started getting serious about implementing the things I've talked to you about in this book. I started thinking in terms of decades rather than months or years.

I just put one foot in front of the other, little by little, step by step—learning what works and what doesn't as I went. I did my best to stop focusing on what I thought success should look like and was determined to seek God's Kingdom as best as I could, trusting that His plan for my life would be better than any plan I could come up with. I just did my best to get out of God's way and let Him lead me.

Recently, I realized that I'm currently living many of the hopes and dreams I had for our family. Our life is simple and without frills, but it's filled with purpose and meaning and fulfillment. I say that as humbly as possible, because here's the thing: When I stopped focusing on my hopes and dreams and instead focused on doing my best with what was in front of me, I actually got the hopes and dreams I had surrendered!

I can really say with certainty and through personal experience: "Delight yourself in the Lord, and he will give you the desires of your heart."[9] Some of the desires I'm seeing fulfilled now are dreams I had for my life; others were new desires God put in me that were what I actually wanted without realizing it. And that's the nature of seeking God's Kingdom—you get what you really needed and find it's what you really wanted.

I'm certain that's what God has for you, too. But it comes slowly, at the speed of a seed.

I pray that this book has given you some practical steps you can take to prioritize what God values in each season of your life. I pray that you'll consistently and unwaveringly seek His Kingdom and His righteousness and that as you do, you will find fulfillment and purpose. God has a good plan for you that will be full of love and joy and peace and goodness. His burden is light—and we'll discover that as we stay focused on putting His Kingdom first.

If you don't see this kind of life yet, don't give up. Stay faithful and trust the process. Implement some of the practices we've talked about in this book. Adapt them to your unique situation. Then stay faithful on the path—one step at a time—because "the path of the righteous is like the light of dawn, which shines brighter and brighter until full day."[10] Brighter and lighter days are ahead, my friends. Count on it!

And let us not grow weary of doing good, for in due season we will reap, if we do not give up. (Galatians 6:9)

Notes

1: Keeping It Light
1. Matthew 11:30
2. Matthew 11:28–30
3. Acts 14:22 NIV
4. Ephesians 6:10 NIV
5. Romans 5:3–4
6. Proverbs 29:18
7. Luke 12:34

2: Priorities
1. Genesis 4:6–7
2. Ecclesiastes 3:1–8
3. Matthew 6:31–33 NIV
4. Colossians 1:16
5. Romans 12:1 NIV
6. John 3:16, my paraphrase

3: Focus

1. Proverbs 29:18
2. C. S. Lewis, *The Weight of Glory* (Grand Rapids, Michigan: Eerdmans Publishing Company, 1949), 2.
3. Psalm 37:4
4. Ephesians 3:20
5. Ephesians 2:10
6. Matthew 25:14–30
7. Matthew 25:27
8. 2 Peter 1:3 NIV
9. "Pareto principle," Wikipedia, https://en.wikipedia.org/wiki/Pareto_principle.

4: Responsibility

1. Francois de La Rochefoucauld, *Maxims*, trans. Stéphane Douard (Seedbox Press, 2011).
2. Matthew 11:29–30 NIV
3. 1 Samuel 18:29 NIV
4. Romans 8:11
5. James 2:17
6. 1 Timothy 6:6
7. Quoted in Robert McKee, *Story: Style, Structure, Substance, and the Principles of Screenwriting* (New York: Reagan Books, 1997), 133.
8. 2 Corinthians 12:9
9. Original quote by Reinhold Neibuhr as part of a longer prayer (ca. 1932). It has since been adopted by Alcoholics Anonymous and used in their literature and training.

5: Margin

1. Reportedly said by Saint Augustine and often quoted by Gerald May.
2. *Merriam-Webster*, s.v. "slave," accessed August 9, 2023, https://www.merriam-webster.com/dictionary/slave.
3. Galatians 5:1 NIV
4. Romans 6:17–18 NIV
5. Psalm 90:12
6. Teresa M. Amabile, Constance Noonan Hadley, and Steven J. Kramer, "Creativity under the Gun," *Harvard Business Review* (August 2002), https://hbr.org/2002/08/creativity-under-the-gun.
7. Jacquelyn Smith, "72% of People Get Their Best Ideas in the Shower—Here's Why," Business Insider, January 14, 2016, https://www.businessinsider.com/why-people-get-their-best-ideas-in-the-shower-2016-1.
8. Deuteronomy 5:14–15 NIV
9. Chris Weller, "Japan Is Facing a 'Death by Overwork' Problem—Here's What It's All About," Business Insider, October 18, 2017, https://www.businessinsider.com/what-is-karoshi-japanese-word-for-death-by-overwork-2017-10.

6: Boundaries

1. Galatians 6:2
2. Matthew 13:36
3. Matthew 7:6
4. Matthew 15:25–28
5. Romans 1:16
6. Acts 10

7. Matthew 15:26

8. Proverbs 22:28 NIV

9. Genesis 2:24

10. Justin Taylor, "Tozer's Contradiction and His Approach to Piety," The Gospel Coalition, June 9, 2008, https://www.thegospelcoalition.org/blogs/justin-taylor/tozers-contradiction-and-his-approach_08.

11. Hebrews 13:4 NIV

12. 1 Corinthians 15:33

13. Galatians 6:2

14. Shawn Achor as quoted by Eric Barker in *Barking up the Wrong Tree: The Surprising Science behind Why Everything You Know about Success Is (Mostly) Wrong* (New York: Harper One, 2017), Kindle.

7: Self-Discovery

1. Proverbs 20:5

2. Galatians 5:1, NIV

3. Matthew 6:31–33

4. Psalm 139:23 NIV

5. Carl Jung letter to Mr. McCullen, *Letters of C. G. Jung*, vol. 2, 1951-1961 (London: Routledge, 1976), quoted on "Carl Jung: Where Your Fear Is, There Is Your Task!!!," Carl Jung Depth Psychology, July 21, 2020, https://carljungdepthpsychologysite.blog/2020/07/21/carl-jung-where-your-fear-is-there-is-your-task.

6. 1 Corinthians 15:10

7. Matthew 16:24

8. Ephesians 2:8–10

8: Consistency

1. Proverbs 13:12 NIV
2. Mark 4:26–29
3. Hebrews 12:11 NIV
4. Ecclesiastes 7:8
5. Galatians 6:9
6. Quoted by Viktor Frankl in *Man's Search for Meaning* (1946), paraphrasing Friedrich Nietzsche from *Twilight of the Idols, or How to Philosophize with a Hammer* (1889).
7. Matthew 25:23
8. 2 Corinthians 10:12
9. Psalm 37:4
10. Proverbs 4:18